*The Observer's Pocket Series*

# FLOWERING TREES & SHRUBS

# Observer's Books

**NATURAL HISTORY**
Birds · Birds' Eggs · Wild Animals · Zoo Animals
Farm Animals · Freshwater Fishes · Sea Fishes
Tropical Fishes · Butterflies · Larger Moths · Insects
Pond Life · Sea and Seashore · Seashells · Dogs
Horses and Ponies · Cats · Pets · Trees · Wild Flowers
Grasses · Mushrooms · Lichens · Garden Flowers
Cacti · Flowering Shrubs · House Plants
Vegetables · Geology · Fossils · Weather · Astronomy

**SPORT**
Soccer · Cricket · Golf · Coarse Fishing
Fly Fishing · Show Jumping · Motor Sport

**TRANSPORT**
Automobiles · Aircraft · Commercial Vehicles · Ships
Motorcycles · Steam Locomotives · Small Craft
Manned Spaceflight · Unmanned Spaceflight

**ARCHITECTURE**
Architecture · Churches · Cathedrals

**COLLECTING**
Awards and Medals · Coins · Postage Stamps
Glass · Pottery and Porcelain · Firearms

**ARTS AND CRAFTS**
Music · Painting · Modern Art · Furniture · Sewing
Jazz · Big Bands

**HISTORY AND GENERAL INTEREST**
Ancient Britain · Flags · Heraldry · European Costume

**TRAVEL**
London · Tourist Atlas GB · Lake District
Cotswolds and Shakespeare Country

# The Observer's Book of
# FLOWERING
# TREES & SHRUBS
## FOR GARDENS

STANLEY B. WHITEHEAD

DESCRIBING OVER 150 GENERA
ILLUSTRATED IN COLOUR

FREDERICK WARNE
LONDON

© Frederick Warne & Co Ltd
London, England
1972

REPRINTED 1974
REPRINTED 1979

LIBRARY OF CONGRESS CATALOG

CARD NO 74–186752

ISBN 0 7232 1506 5

Printed in Great Britain by
William Clowes & Sons, Limited
London, Beccles and Colchester
05775.179

# CONTENTS

# PREFACE

In preparing this shorter version of *The Book of Flowering Trees and Shrubs* I have endeavoured to select and present the pick of these plants which are the most beautiful and the most rewarding for growing out of doors in the smaller gardens of today, and which are in commercial production and offered by our British nurseries. It is, necessarily, a concise guide to over 150 genera and their finest varieties and hybrids. But with Miss Joan Lupton's illustrations to show quality and aid identification, and precise plant descriptions, up-to-date names, and cultural notes, I hope it may prove a very useful tool for the gardener to have at hand in his pocket, and be found worthy of the *Observer's Series*.

SBW

# INTRODUCTION

## Shrubs in the Modern Garden

Botanically, shrubs are perennial plants with several woody, separate and persistent stems growing from or near the base. Together with single-stemmed trees of short stature, they become the permanent ornamental furnishings of the modern garden. The initial cost of shrubs is heavy, but subsequent care and management are sparing of time and effort.

The most important points to have in mind, when choosing them, are their size, particularly their height and breadth when mature, and their habit of growth. In small gardens shrubs may be interplanted among flowers in a bed or a border, concentrating on shrubs which are not only floriferous in themselves but possessed of good foliage to furnish the border and to contrast with the herbaceous or other flowers in their season. The place of the specimen tree may be more suitably filled by the ornamental shrub. The taller-growing shrubs are ideal for lawns, for the end of a vista, and for forecourts. Flowering or berrying shrubs in tubs or vases may be used on paved terraces, forecourts or in circumscribed town gardens.

**Shrub Borders**  The real art of shrub gardening, however, lies in using these plants in a border, belt or group planned as a composite and complete unity. It is better to concentrate on a few of the best genera and species of shrubs than to attempt to embrace them all. One way is to group like species and varieties together. For example, the grouping of Heaths and Heathers makes a colourful display in season, while the foliage of these shrubs is not unpleasing at other times.

Other genera which offer scope for group planting are *Rhododendron* and its *Azalea* section, *Berberis*, *Genista*, *Cistus*, *Helianthemum*, *Rosa*, *Hydrangea*, *Potentilla*, *Escallonia* and *Hebe*.

In planning the shrubbery proper, however, over-crowding is an evil to avoid. Each individual plant should have sufficient room to develop naturally and to reach a mature size. It can then display its true quality.

Modern gardens are the out-door living rooms of the home. The nearer to the buildings that shrubs are planted, the more important it is to use those of apt size and shape; correctly chosen, shrubs can help 'fit' a house into its setting as few other plants can.

The design of a shrub garden must necessarily be subordinate to the space available. It should, however, be planned on informal, natural lines. The sweeping curve, the round or the irregularly elliptical edge to borders or beds is more fitting to the natural habit of ornamental shrubs than the straight line, square or rectangle. There should be some irregularity in their placing and a complete avoidance of anything approaching regimentation.

In shrub gardening, the tree should be considered subordinate to the shrub. The trees which fit in best are those which cast only light shade, and which are of a stature suitable for the garden. A sensible limit is to plant no tree that has a height greater than one-third that of the greatest dimension of the garden.

The abbreviations **Sh**, **T**, **Cl Sh** indicate Shrub, Tree or Climbing Shrub.

# Soils and Situations

Before choosing the shrubs we should like to grow, some consideration should be given to the soil and the situation in which they are to be planted.

**The Nature of Soils**    The soil is the medium in which the shrub anchors itself by means of its roots and the source of various plant foods or nutrients, which consist of a range of mineral salts dissolved in the water which is present in all soils.    The plant absorbs them through fine hair-like rootlets. Garden soils are made up of five components: (1) the inorganic mineral fraction; (2) the organic fraction; (3) air; (4) water; (5) soil life.    The mineral matter consists of particles fragmented by weathering and other natural forces from various kinds of rock. The finest particles are microscopic, lying so closely together as to adhere easily, and are termed clay.    The coarser particles consist of sands, gravel and stones.    Between the finest sand and coarsest clay come intermediate particles known as silt.

The kind and proportion of particles in a soil determine its texture.    A soil containing more than 15% clay is apt to be sticky, to hold water and to be heavy to work.    Soils containing much sand, gravel or stones drain freely, can be cultivated easily and are called light.    Silt soils are of an intermediate texture without the stickiness of clay. Since fine particles are more easily decomposed than coarse ones, clay soils are potentially richer in soluble plant foods than sandy ones.

The organic fraction of a soil consists of the decaying remains of plants and animals which are broken down to a substance known as humus and soluble nutrients for plants.    The addition of humus-forming organic matter to the inert mineral earth creates a living soil.

Humus is the state of organic matter in the soil

when it reaches the last stages of decomposition; amorphous, brown to black colour, and a weak cement, binding soil particles together, to make all soils more granular or crumbed. It is colloidal, absorbing moisture and becomes a reservoir for soluble plant food. Humus lightens the texture of clay while increasing the ability of sands to hold moisture.

Air and water occupy the spaces between the particles of the soil. Both are essential to the biochemistry of soil and plant nutrition. They should, however, be present in good balance. Too much water and too little air means a cold wet soil in which plant roots may rot.

The soil life is floral and faunal. There are tiny algae, lichens and fungi in the soil, living out their life cycles, and in decay adding to its humus. Fungi break down added organic matter and may help in the feeding of plants. The most important soil organisms, however, are the bacteria of which it is estimated more than 2,000,000,000 may be found in a salt-spoonful of soil.

Together with fungi, bacteria feed on organic remains in the soil and are responsible for their decomposition. There are bacteria which fix nitrogen from the air, bacteria which convert complex nitrogenous compounds into nitrates which plants can use, and bacteria which free other plant foods from organic material and from the mineral particles of the soil.

Other soil organisms include beneficial earthworms and nematodes which tunnel the soil to improve its aeration and drainage and to mix mineral and organic fractions together. The soil may also be frequented by various fungi, eel-worms, insects and animals parasitic on other organisms or plants. Under good cultivation, however, such parasites can be controlled.

As a result of the inter-activity between these

five constituents the soil water becomes a dilute solution of the soluble salts available, on which plant roots feed.

Just how well plants can exploit the soil solution depends partly upon its acid-alkaline balance as it governs the kind and quantity of nutrients which a plant can use. In garden soils, this balance is usually governed by the presence or absence of lime, and is measured by what is called $pH$ scale.

On the $pH$ scale $pH$ 7 indicates a neutral solution. Ratings lower than 7 indicate acidity; ratings higher than 7 indicate alkalinity. The $pH$ rating of any soil is an indication of its hydrogen-ion concentration, and this can be detected electrically with great accuracy, or more simply and approximately, though accurately enough for gardening purposes, by observing the reactions of special dye solutions to the soil. Such solutions are available in inexpensive Soil Testing Outfits for gardeners.

Most garden plants grow best in acid to slightly acid soils of $pH$ 5·5 to 6·5, and ornamental shrubs tolerate and like a soil $pH$ of 5 to 6·5. Acidity is corrected by adding lime, the amount depending upon the degree of acidity to be corrected and the kind of lime used. Alkalinity is more difficult to correct, requiring the use of sulphur, peat, organic manures and acid-reacting fertilizers.

In considering soils suitable for ornamental shrubs a clear distinction must be drawn between the soils which contain lime and the soils which are lime-free. The presence of lime, even in an acid soil, is not tolerated by certain genera, particularly those of the Ericaceae, itemed under *Peat Soils* later in this chapter.

**Clay Soils** The characteristics of clay soils are tenacity, plasticity when wet, heaviness to cultivate, and tendency to lie wet and cold. Most clay soils, unless the clay is of the type known as marl, are also acid. To improve them, clay soils require horticultural gypsum at $\frac{1}{2}$–1 lb per square yard initially, followed by liberal dressings of humus-forming organic material, chiefly rotted manure, compost, horticultural peat, leafmould, spent hops, chopped straw or bracken, forked into the top-soil when the soil is roughly dug in the autumn or early winter. If strongly acid, lime may follow in the winter, using ground limestone at 8 to 12 oz per square yard.

The addition of coarse sand, coke breeze, gravel, etc., is helpful to improve texture, but can only be attempted in a small way. What is more important is to see that the drainage is good. With good drainage and humus-enrichment, most ornamental shrubs can be grown on clay soils.

**Sandy Soils** have an openness of texture, free drainage, a quick response to temperature changes and a tendency to dry out. Such soils lose their soluble elements rapidly in drainage and so tend to be of poor fertility. They are, however, light and easy to work. Their primary need is organic matter—animal manures, shoddy, peat, compost, spent hops, leafmould, etc.—forked into the top spit in winter and applied as mulching in summer. If easily obtainable, a ton or two of clay to the rod, spread roughly on the surface to weather in during winter, greatly increases moisture-holding for many years. Organic fertilizers are most helpful in building up fertility. Acid sands are best amended by the addition of ground chalk, since this material absorbs a little moisture.

As the moisture-holding capacity and the fertility of the soil are increased, a wide range of ornamental plants can be grown.

**Calcareous Soils** overlie chalk, limestone or marl. They contain carbonate of lime in abundance, and this makes them alkaline. To grow shrubs well, it is necessary to neutralize this alkalinity. The first essential is good drainage so that soluble lime salts are leached. Any hard or solid sub-soil rock or pan should be broken by pick or mattock. The tendency is for the top soil to lose lime to the sub-soil, and it should not be brought back again.

The second need is to dress liberally with organic matter. Animal manures, compost, peat, shoddy, leafmould, sewage and green manure material are all useful. Acid-reacting fertilizers such as dried blood, sulphate of ammonia and sulphate of potash can be used with advantage.

Excessive alkalinity tends to deny iron to plants and a common symptom of iron starvation in plants growing on calcareous soils is the paling of the foliage known as chlorosis.

Other nutrients may also be held unavailable, and growth is thereby stunted. The modern counter is to feed plants with chelated compounds of iron, etc. (Sequestrenes) periodically.

Given adequate organic manuring, the range of shrubs which can be grown on chalk, limestone and the lighter marl soils is quite extensive.

**Peat Soils** are usually found on moorlands on heaths overlying poor sand or stony soil, and in the Fens. Such soils are moisture-retentive, inclined to be deficient in potash, and are not at first highly fertile. Exposure of the peat to the air and weather aids its further decomposition; a process which can be fostered by drainage, where the peat soil is a wet one, by the addition of animal manures or compost and fertilizers, and if desirable by liming.

In shrub-growing, however, a peaty soil is ideal for the calcifuge plants which hate lime. These include some of the most beautiful genera in cultivation, such as:

| | |
|---|---|
| *Arbutus* species | *Camellia* species |
| *Calluna* species | *Cassiope* species |

| | |
|---|---|
| *Daboecia* species | *Pieris* species |
| *Enkianthus* species | *Rhododendron* species |
| *Erica* species | *Stewartia* species |
| *Gaultheria* species | *Styrax* species |
| *Kalmia* species | *Vaccinium* species |
| *Pernettya* species | *Zenobia* species |

With cultivation and the addition of lime, peat soils may also be planted with many other shrubs to vary the planting scheme.

**Silt Soils** Silt particles are finer than sand, yet coarser than clay, and soils rich in silt are often difficult since they do not drain freely nor do they have the stickiness of clay. They are apt to become compacted and inert in cultivation, and do not react to lime in the same way that clay does. The chief need of silt soils in shrub-growing is organic matter. Once this is assured, silt soils can be as productive as any other.

Their precise treatment, however, depends upon whether the texture is coarse or fine. A coarse silt soil will also contain sand, and is best cultivated on the lines suggested for a sandy soil. A fine, heavy silt soil is usually admixed with clay and may be treated and amended as a clay soil. The same criterion can be applied in deciding the most suitable shrubs to plant.

**Situation** Shrubs that are native to foreign countries can only thrive in our gardens where climatic conditions are broadly similar to those of their native habitat. Latitude, altitude and geographical situation must be taken into account when choosing shrubs. Geographical position whether coastal or inland, in the damper west or the drier east, whether facing north, south, east or west, will have a bearing in determining which shrubs will thrive and which ones will not.

Apart from the general climate, each garden has

a local climate, according to the lie of the land and its relation to its surroundings. Such matters as shade and sun, nearness to towns or industrial areas, exposure to wind and frost and the actual terrain within the garden must influence the choice of plants for specific locations.

**Frost-susceptible situations** Severe winter frosts may cause plant losses almost anywhere in Britain, but the greatest damage is done by un-timely frosts in spring when the plants are freshly coming into growth.

Cold air, being heavier than warm, collects at and near ground level and flows over the contours of the ground to the lowest parts. Consequently, gardens in valleys, on low-lying ground, or in pockets are most likely to sustain spring frost damage. Here it is wise to plant the hardiest of shrubs and to ensure a good show species and varieties which flower when the danger of frost is past.

**Windy situations** Wind may sometimes be formidable for its mechanical force but far more for its climatic effect. Wind accentuates the effect of the climatic conditions in which it blows. Winds coinciding with spring frost increase the cold's deadliness. The art of minimizing the effect of wind lies in breaking its force up into minor turbulences. A trellis or openwork fence or boundary planting of suitable shrubs or trees is more effective than an impenetrable obstruction.

No shrubs are draught-proof, but for exposed situations, the following are useful as a first line of defence against winds:

*Crataegus oxyacantha*      *Prunus cerasifera*
*Hippophae rhamnoides*      *Prunus spinosa*
*Ilex aquifolium*      *Sambucus nigra*
*Ligustrum ovalifolium*      *Tamarix gallica*
*Lonicera yunnanensis*      *Ulex europaeus*
*Olearia haastii*

For gardens on the coast where winds are often laden with salt spray, the following are more suitable:

> *Escallonia macrantha* and vars
> *Euonymus* species
> *Hippophae rhamnoides*
> *Senecio rotundifolius*
> *Tamarix tetrandra*

**Shady situations**   All green plants are dependent on light for their nutrition and energy but vary in the amount of light they need or can tolerate. Broadly it may be said that the plants which do best in full sun are those with softish leaves well equipped with pores (stomata) and an internal structure through which carbon dioxide gas diffuses quickly.   Plants which can tolerate and grow in shade are those with rather tough, darkish leaf structure that diffuses $CO_2$ slowly.

**Dry situations**   Plants which can stoutly resist both the limiting effects of a parched dry soil and an exposed site such as on a terrace, bank or wall, are chiefly to be sought among the grey or narrow-leaved shrubs such as:

| | |
|---|---|
| *Cistus* species | *Rosmarinus officinalis* |
| *Cotoneaster microphylla* | *Santolina* species |
| *Cytisus* species | *Spartium junceum* |
| *Genista* species | *Tamarix* species |
| *Helianthemum* species | *Ulex europaeus* |
| *Lavandula* species | |

**Wet situations**   No shrubs will thrive in waterlogged conditions where the water is stagnant, but the following can be planted with confidence by water and in wet situations from which the water does drain, if slowly:

| | |
|---|---|
| *Cornus* species | *Skimmia* species |
| *Kalmia* species | *Vaccinium* species |
| *Salix* species | |

# Planting and Propagation

Good planting ensures the rapid recovery of the shrub from the shock of moving, and preserves the future good shape and symmetry of the shrub. Most garden soils can be best prepared by bastard trenching, a thorough turning over of the top spit and a breaking up of the second spit or sub-soil where it lies.

**Soil Treatment before Planting**  Thoroughly rooted organic matter, manure or compost, or moist peat, should be worked into the top soil. Artificial fertilizers are not desirable.  Bone meal is safe and helpful on most soils.  On light hungry soils, sulphate of potash will aid rooting action and strengthen disease resistance.

**Planting Time**  Deciduous shrubs and trees may be planted out in mild weather, when the soil is workable, from late October to early April. Evergreen shrubs should be moved either in early autumn, from September to November, or from mid-March to May.

Some shrubs do not move well and are consequently usually grown in pots and containers or can be planted almost at any time of the year except during weather extremes.  Trees and shrubs received from the nursery during a period of frost or when the soil is too waterlogged for planting are best placed in a shallow trench at a slanting angle of 45°, their roots heaped over with soil until *favourable* planting conditions return.

**Stock for Planting**  Shrubs and trees transplant most easily when young, and in choosing stock for planting, preference is best given to juvenile plants of sturdy growth, well furnished with fibrous roots.

**Planting Technique**  The planting hole should

be dug at least one-third again as wide as the spread of the roots. If the sub-soil has not been broken up previously this should be done and the soil re-firmed.

Most shrubs and trees should be planted to the same soil level as they have been growing. The roots should be carefully spread out as evenly as possible, and each root must be firmly embraced by the loamy compost, and soil should be worked into the interstices of the root system with the hands before finally topping to soil level and watering well. A mulch of organic litter is then spread over the rooting area, leaving the soil around the base of the plant clear.

Plants moved with roots in a ball of soil may be soaked in water prior to planting.

Support against wind-rocking for trees and large shrubs in exposed positions may be obtained by stakes driven into the soil before filling the planting hole. The ties should be loose enough to allow for growth expansion of the *stem*.

**Propagation** Shrubs may be propagated by seeds or by methods of vegetative reproduction, such as by taking cuttings or by layering.

**Shrubs from Seeds** Shrubs raised from seeds usually develop into healthy, longlived plants. They do, however, take rather a long time growing to flowering age and good size. Only general principles can be given here, while special indications for species requiring different techniques are given in the main text of the book.

The seeds should be fully ripe, especially when home-saved. The normal time to sow is in the late winter or spring months. Seed capsules, berries, etc., should be collected when ripe and stored under cool, dry conditions until required. Seed berries or fruits are best layered between layers of damp sand in boxes, and the seeds later rubbed out from the pulp when sowing time arrives.

To germinate well, seeds need only air, moisture and warmth. Temperatures for germination run rather higher than those necessary for the growth of the seedling and plant. Air and moisture are provided by choosing a suitable soil and sowing the seeds at the correct depth.

Broadly, seeds of shrubs native to temperate zones similar in climate to our own can be sown out of doors, preferably in prepared seed beds of free-draining sandy loam in a warm sheltered location in the garden. Seeds of tropical or sub-tropical species usually need to be sown under glass with the stimulus of artificial heat. Seeds of alpine species and those native to cold climates may need to be subjected to the actions of frost and snow before germinating successfully.

To have the process of germination under careful watch and control, the seeds may be sown in boxes, pots or pans, subsequently stood in propagating cases, greenhouses or cold frames according to the conditions required. The soil compost should be a modern soilless compost or the John Innes Seeds Compost consisting of:

3 parts by bulk of sterilized loam
2 parts by bulk of sedge or moss peat
1 part by bulk of coarse sand plus
1½ oz of superphosphate and ¾ oz of ground chalk or ground limestone per bushel of mixed compost.

For lime-hating species like *Erica* and *Rhodo-dendron* the chalk or limestone should be omitted.

The depth at which to sow seeds is roughly twice their diameter. Germination time varies. In some species it may take several months. Where there is some risk of the seeds drying out before they germinate it is helpful to cover the surface of the compost with a layer of finely chopped moist sphagnum moss and sow the seeds in this.

After germination, seedlings may grow rapidly. Those already out of doors should be allowed to complete a season of growth before being moved. Those in seed containers may be carefully transplanted to a richer soil compost in pots when they have made their first true leaves, and later hardened off until the season is appropriate to plant them out of doors.

**Vegetative Propagation** This enables us to reproduce plants identical with the parent plant, and to multiply a desirable plant quickly. The simplest method is by means of 'cuttings'—portions of the stems or shoots, or roots, or leaves.

**Stem cuttings** Cuttings of the stem or shoot are of three kinds according to when they are taken; 'hardwood' cuttings, 'softwood' cuttings, or half-ripe cuttings with a 'heel'.

*Hardwood cuttings* are taken in autumn. They are cut cleanly from firm, healthy lateral shoots of the current season's growth, with four to six buds, cut a little below a node. The cuttings are inserted in a bed of sandy loam, shaded and sheltered, with the top bud only above ground. They root very rapidly under bell glasses or cloches, and may be left to grow for a year before being moved to permanent quarters.

*Softwood cuttings* consist of portions of growing greenwood lateral shoots with a terminal bud or growing point, taken in early or mid-summer when firm. The lower leaves are cut off, and the cuttings, usually a few inches long, inserted in a suitable soil under close conditions. In the case of some species, cuttings root readily enough when inserted in light, well-drained soil out of doors under bell-glasses or even in jam-jars. But for consistent results it is best to root softwood cuttings in a mist propagating case where transpiration can be carefully controlled and the best conditions for rooting maintained.

The cuttings are inserted and firmed in along their length, and are kept moist and close until rooted, when more ventilation is needed.

*Cuttings with a heel* are generally the most successful. They consist of half-ripened lateral shoots of the current year's growth detached with the base or 'heel' of the older wood at their junction with the stem, in summer. The heel should be trimmed of ragged tissue and the leaves removed from the lower end. The cuttings are then inserted in sandy soil out of doors, in partial shade, and given the protection of a bell-glass, handlight, cloche or jam-jar to prevent undue moisture loss. Such cuttings root readily inserted around the rim of a flower-pot, or a cold frame. Heeled cuttings may also be propagated in a propagating case or frame as for softwood cuttings.

Stem cuttings vary in the time they take to root or 'strike'. Rooting can, however, be quickened by treating the cuttings beforehand with one of the root-inducing growth-regulating substances or synthetic hormones. Broadly, shrubs with hollow or pithy stems are more difficult to root from cuttings than those with solid stems.

**Root cuttings** A few species are easily propagated by root cuttings, chiefly those which produce suckers easily. The method entails cutting the roots into 2-in. lengths, inserting them in moist sand or cuttings compost, about $\frac{1}{2}$ in. deep, with the plant end uppermost, in pots. *Rhus*, *Fatsia*, *Campsis* and *Yucca* can be propagated in this way.

**Leaf Cuttings** Very few shrubs are propagated by leaf cuttings. Camellias may be treated this way, however. The cutting consists of about an inch section of the stem with a leaf and axillary bud on it. The stem is removed by half or two-thirds its thickness and with the bud just below the surface of the compost. Such cuttings are taken in late summer or early autumn.

**Layering**  Shrubs which do not root readily from cuttings may often be propagated by layering. To soil-layer a shrub, a low or pendent branch is chosen which will easily reach the ground about a foot or so from the tip. A hole is made about 4 in. to 8 in. deep to take the branch when bent.

Rooting is induced by a partial disruption of the sap flow at the lowest point of the bent shoot. If the shoot is acutely bent to form a U without cracking, this is sufficient. It can be pegged down to the bottom of the hole and covered with soil, the upright end being staked and about 6 in. above ground. Other ways of checking the sap flow are: notching the underside of the shoot; making a slanting slit to cut the shoot half-way through below a bud in an upward direction towards the apex; ringing, by removing a ring of bark about $\frac{1}{2}$ in. wide; or by wiring, which calls for twisting a piece of wire tightly around the stem. In each case, the prepared layer is pegged down, covered with fine soil, and kept moist with about 6 in. of the free end of the shoot projecting. Layering is best done in spring or early summer. The layered shoot is then left until well rooted, when it can be severed from the parent plant and transplanted the following autumn, but slow rooting species may take two years.

With shrubs which have few or no branches which can be layered in the soil, air-layering can be attempted. A chosen upright shoot is split, ringed or notched at the point where rooting is desired. If split, a small pebble or piece of matchstick or wire should be inserted to keep the split open. The point of injury is then enclosed in a poultice of moist sphagnum moss wrapped in a sleeve of polythene film, taped at each end.

In all layering, rooting can be speeded up by painting the point of sap interruption with one of the root-inducing, growth-regulating substances used for cuttings.

Many shrubs and trees are vegetatively propagated by budding in summer and grafting in spring by techniques outside the scope of this book.

## The Care of Trees and Shrubs

The newly planted shrub or tree during the first season of new growth will be preoccupied in establishing its roots, and beyond watering in dry spells, no attempts to feed or fertilize should be made. Thereafter the care of the shrub garden is largely a matter of pruning and manuring.

**Pruning** Properly arranged and well cultivated, most shrubs do best without regular pruning. Pruning is, however, often helpful in shaping young plants, and it is practical to prune shrubs of no particular beauty as far as shape is concerned but which are esteemed for their flowers. Then there are the shrubs which need renovation.

**How to prune** Hard pruning tends to provoke strong new shoots or wood growth, light pruning to foster flowering. Good pruning should hardly show, unwanted shoots being cut either to just above a bud facing the direction new growth is desired, or at the base flush with the junction of an older branch or stem. The general habit of the species, whether upright, arching, pyramidal, bushy or sprawling, should be taken into consideration.

Cuts should be made with the sharpest of knives or secateurs, giving preference to tools which do the least damage to the bark. Large cut surfaces are best dressed with a tree antiseptic (Arbrex 805) to keep out parasitic fungi and decay.

25

**When to prune** Decaying, dead or diseased growth should be removed as soon as it is seen, and burnt. Evergreen shrubs usually need very little pruning while in healthy and pleasing growth. When it is desired to cut overgrown branches back, the work should be done in spring, giving the new growth the longest season possible to mature.

Deciduous shrubs should be pruned according to their flowering habit. They may be divided into two kinds. First, those shrubs which flower on shoots of the previous year, including the winter-and-spring-flowering species, should be pruned as soon as flowering is over.

Second, those shrubs which flower on shoots grown during the current year and flower in summer or autumn should be pruned in the spring when the sap is rising, when the old wood which has flowered can be cut out severely if so desired. Suckers of shrubs, such as *Syringa* (Lilac), should be twisted off the roots in spring.

Most ornamental trees only need pruning to maintain a clear stem and well balanced branching head. Deciduous trees may be pruned when it is convenient.

Some trees, notably the Birch and Maple, bleed readily if cut when the sap is rising in late winter or spring. Such species should be pruned in full leaf. In the case of species of *Prunus*, such as flowering Almonds, Peaches, Plums and Cherries, there is a danger of gumming if cut too severely and too early in the year and of Silver Leaf Disease infection if pruned too late. The best time to prune these is June to July, certainly not later than August.

**Manuring** Regular digging is undesirable, since many shrubs have fine feeding roots near the surface. It is sufficient to prick over the soil in autumn or early winter, removing weeds and debris, and then apply a mulch.

The mulch may consist of wetted and partially rotted leaves, rotted vegetable compost, peat, chopped bracken or chopped clean straw, applied evenly to cover the soil to a depth of 2 in. to 4 in. Sawdust may be used, though a depth of 1 in. to 2 in. is sufficient. In summer, the soil can be mulched with lawn mowings or any suitable organic material to hand.

The use of artificial fertilizers around shrubs needs care. On the whole, it is wise to use the organic fertilizers as far as possible if and when extra feeding is necessary.

For the shrub garden, a mixture of 2 parts by weight hoof and horn meal, 4 parts bone meal, and 2 parts powdered seaweed applied at 4 to 6 oz per square yard every third or fourth year under the annual mulch, will be found to promote balanced and healthy growth.

# GLOSSARY

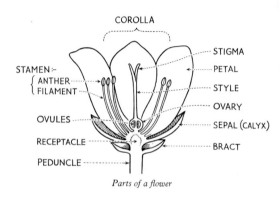

*Parts of a flower*

**Acute**   ending in a point; sharp.
**Alternate**   of leaves, arranged not opposite or whorled, but in rows or spirally, not more than one at a node.
**Anther**   the pollen-bearing part of the stamen.
**Axil**   upper angle formed by junction of leaf and stem.
**Axillary**   growing in the axil.

**Blade**   expanded part of a leaf or petal
**Bract**   a modified leaf growing near the calyx of a flower.

**Calcicole**   lime-tolerant, usually growing in soils containing free lime.
**Calcifuge**   lime-intolerant, usually growing in acid, lime-free soils.
**Calyx**   the outer whorl of floral envelopes, or sepals.
**Capsule**   a dry fruit composed of more than one carpel.
**Carpel**   one of the units or divisions of a pistil.
**Catkin**   a dense, scaly-bracted spike, usually composed of unisexual, petal-less flowers.

**Chlorophyll**   the green colouring matter of plants.

**Compound**   of a leaf, made up of separate leaflets; of an inflorescence, with the axis branched; of a pistil, with two or more carpels united.

**Compressed**   flattened.

**Cordate**   heart-shaped.

**Corolla**   the petals of a flower.

**Corymb**   a cluster of stalked flowers arising from different levels but with pedicels so adjusted in length that the flowers make a flat-topped head.

**Cyme**   a branching inflorescence of which the central flower opens first with lateral branches which also have terminal flowers.

**Deciduous**   falling-off, of plants losing their leaves in autumn.

**Dentate**   with sharp teeth directed outwards.

**Digitate**   hand-like. *See* **Palmate**.

**Dioecious**   having the sexes on different plants.

**Disk, Disc**   the fleshy part of the receptacle of a flower, surrounding or surmounting the pistil or ovary.

**Drupe**   a more or less fleshy fruit, with one or more seeds enclosed in a stony layer or endocarp.

**Elongate**   stretched out; lengthened.

**Entire**   of leaves, having continuous margin, uncut and without teeth.

**Evergreen**   of plants which retain their foliage green for at least a full year, remaining green throughout their dormant season.

**Fastigiate**   having erect branches, close together.

**Fertilization**   the process of union between male and female gametes, or reproductive cells.

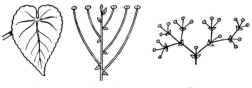

*Cordate*          *Corymb*                    *Cyme*

**Filament**  the stalk of the anther.  *See* **Stamen**.

**Florets**  small individual flowers, especially those in heads as of the Compositae.

**Floriferous**  flower-bearing; producing many flowers.

**Fruit**  the seed-bearing organ, usually implies the ripe seeds and adnate structure, whether pulpy or dry.

**Genus; Genera**  a group of species with common structural characters.

**Gland**  a small vesicle containing oil, resin, chalk, sugar or other liquid, in, on or protruding from the surface of any part of a plant.

**Glaucous**  bluish or grey, with a waxy bloom.

**Hermaphrodite**  containing stamens and ovary.

**Hybrid**  the offspring of the fertilization of one species by another usually indicated by the sign ×.

**Inflorescence**  the flowering portion and its arrangement, including stalks, bracts and flowers, on the stem.

**Internode**  part of the stem between two nodes.

**Labiate**  lipped.

**Lanceolate**  lance- or spear-shaped; elliptically longer than broad, tapering to both ends.

**Lateral**  on or at the side.

**Lax**  loose, not compact or dense.

**Leaflet**  secondary leaf, part of a compound leaf.

**Linear**  long and narrow, with sides parallel or nearly so.

**Lobe**  a part of an organ, leaf or petal, divided from the rest of it by an indentation.

**Monoecious**  having unisexual flowers, but with both sexes on the same plant.

*Lanceolate*    *Linear*    *Obovate*    *Orbicular*

**Node**   a point or joint on the stem from which one or more leaves arise.

**Obovate**   inversely ovate, with the broader end terminal.
**Obtuse**   blunt, rounded.
**Opposite**   of two leaves or organs arising at the same level on opposite sides of a stem.
**Orbicular**   round or circular, length and breadth about equal.
**Palmate**   divided like a palm or hand, usually of leaves with more than three leaflets arising from the same point.
**Panicle**   a branching racemose inflorescence.
**Pedicel**   the stalk of a single flower.
**Peduncle**   the stalk of a flower-cluster or an inflorescence.
**Perennial**   living for more than two years, and normally flowering each year.
**Perianth**   the outer, non-essential floral organs, including the petals and sepals, when present.
**Petiole**   the stalk of a leaf.
**Pinnate**   having leaflets arranged in two rows along each side of a common stalk or axis.
**Pistil**   the ovule- and seed-bearing organ, consisting of ovary, stigma and style.
**Pistillate**   female, having pistils but no stamens.
**Pollen**   the spores or grains borne by the anther, containing the male element, of a flowering plant.
**Pome**   a many-celled, fleshy fruit (e.g. apple, pear, quince).
**Procumbent**   trailing or lying flat on the surface.
**Prostrate**   lying closely along the surface of the ground.

*Oval*          *Palmate*          *Panicle*          *Raceme*

**Raceme**   a simple, elongated, unbranched inflorescence in which the flowers are borne on pedicels.

**Radical**   of leaves arising from the root or a rhizome.

**Receptacle**   the upper part of the stem from which the parts of the flower arise; the torus.

**Recurved**   bent backward in a curve.

**Reflexed**   abruptly bent backward or downward.

**Rib**   the primary vein of a leaf or other similar organ.

**Rugose**   wrinkled.


**Sagittate**   arrow-shaped, triangular, with basal lobes pointing downwards.

**Scabrous**   rough, especially to the touch.

**Scape**   the flowering stem of a plant with all radical leaves, arising from the root.

**Seed**   a fertilized and ripened ovule.

**Sepal**   one of the separate green leaves of a calyx.

**Shrub**   a woody plant branching freely from the base, remaining low in form.

**Simple**   not compound; an undivided leaf.

**Species**   a group of individuals having the same constant and distinct characters.

**Spike**   a simple inflorescence with the flowers sessile along an unbranched axis.

**Spine**   a stiff, straight, sharp-pointed woody structure, usually arising from the wood of a stem.

**Spore**   a small asexual reproductive body, usually a single cell.

**Spreading**   standing out horizontally.

**Spur**   a hollow tubular or sac-like projection from a blossom, usually secreting nectar.

*Sagittate*　　*Sessile*　　*Spatulate*　　*Spike*

**Stamen**  the male reproductive organ of the plant, consisting of the filament and anther bearing the pollen sacs.

**Stellate**  star-shaped.

**Sterile**  non-productive of seed capable of germination; of anthers not producing viable pollen.

**Stigma**  the receptive surface or part of the pistil which receives the pollen.

**Stipule**  a scale- or leaf-like basal appendage of a petiole, usually in pairs, and sometimes adnate.

**Style**  the part of the pistil connecting the ovary and the stigma.

**Sucker**  a shoot arising adventitiously from the root system of a shrub or tree, often away from the base.

**Terminal**  borne at the end of a stem or branch.

**Tomentose**  densely covered with short cottony hairs.

**Tree**  a woody perennial plant with a single main stem (trunk) and elevated branching head.

**Umbel**  an inflorescence in which the flower-stalks all arise from the top of the main stem and common point, to give an umbrella-shaped head.

**Undulate**  wavy.

**Unisexual**  of one sex.

**Whorl**  three or more leaves or organs of the same kind arising at the same level or node.

*Stipule*          *Umbel*                    *Whorl*

# DESCRIPTION OF
SPECIES

*Abelia*
*× grandiflora*

A genus of attractive deciduous and evergreen shrubs, with arching stems, small, short-stalked, opposite leaves, and pink or white tubular or funnel-shaped flowers. They thrive in any well-drained loamy soil, including limy ones. Generally hardy in southern England and in mild localities, but elsewhere need shelter.

The best species are : *A. floribunda*, an evergreen from Mexico, growing three to five feet tall, with reddish, downy stems, small, toothed, glossy green ovate leaves and rosy magenta, tubular flowers in twos or threes from June. *A. × grandiflora* is a popular hybrid, with arching shoots, up to five feet high, ovate, shallowly toothed leaves, and pink-blush white, funnel-shaped flowers slightly scented, semi-evergreen. *A. schumannii*, China, is deciduous with purplish downy stems, pale-green ovate leaves, and solitary, bell-shaped, rose-pink flowers from June to September, it grows to four feet high. Stems may be killed back in hard winter, but shoot up again in spring. *A. uniflora*, a Chinese evergreen, has handsome flowers, white flushed pink, orange at the throat, and in clusters of two to four, in June.

Propagate by softwood cuttings in July; by 'heeled' cuttings in September and October.

This large genus of trees is notable for its species with brightly and variously tinted autumn foliage. The leaves grow opposite and are long-stalked; the flowers yellowish or whitish green, and the two-winged fruits or keys are characteristic. They flourish in moist, humus-rich, well-drained soils and should be sheltered to preserve the foliage undamaged. *A. gris-eum*, from central China makes a twenty-five to forty foot tree. Its bark peels orange-red. The leaves are trifoliolate, turning orange and bright red in autumn. *A. japonicum*, from Japan, may be grown as a small tree or bushy scrub; its shapely roundish leaves have seven to eleven lobes, var. *aureum* has pale golden foliage and flare ruby crimson in autumn. *A. palmatum*, the Japanese Maple, may make a twenty to forty foot tree with a typical five-lobed and toothed Maple leaf; its var. *atropurpureum* has dark purple foliage, var. *aureum*, yellow turning gold. Vars. *dissectum* form a group with deeply cut lobed leaves. Vars. *septemlobum* has seven-lobed leaves, and *osakazuki* colours magnificently to orange red and scarlet.

*Acer palmatum var. atro-purpureum*

Propagation of species may be attempted by seeds sown out-doors in October, but choice kinds are budded in August, grafted in March.

*Amelanchier
canadensis*

Easily grown and quite hardy, the Amelanchiers are a genus of deciduous shrubs or small trees, attractive for a short time in spring with hanging racemes of five-petalled white flowers but chiefly valued for their autumn colouring when the alternate, roundish, toothed leaves tint beautifully. They do well in ordinary garden loams of good drainage and like the sun.

*A. laevis* of North America is a graceful tree of twenty feet or more, flowering in April. Its leaves, smooth when young, turn red in autumn. Its compatriot, *A. canadensis* (syn. *A. oblongifolia*) flowers at the same time, has young leaves that are downy, colouring magnificently in autumn. Of the shrubby species, *A. ovalis* (syn. *A. vulgaris*) of Europe is the Snowy Mespilus, five to eight feet, with clusters of large white flowers in May and berries black in autumn. The oval leaves are white-felted beneath when young, colouring with age. *A. lamarckii*, a naturalized species of Europe, has silky leaves, lax racemes of white flowers, and rich autumn colours.

Propagate by fresh seeds in autumn; by softwood cuttings in July; by layering in spring; or in the case of shrub species by division in November.

# Arbutus
Family ERICACEAE

In this genus of evergreen shrubs or trees, with alternate, leathery, deep-green leaves, panicles of pitcher-shaped, pendent flowers and colourful, ball-like fruits, *Arbutus unedo*, the Strawberry Tree, of Ireland and southern Europe, is outstanding. It makes a shrub-like tree, ten to thirty feet high, beautiful in foliage with ovate, toothed leaves, charming for its terminal clusters of pinkish-white,

*Arbutus unedo*

pitcher-shaped flowers, which ripen to globular fruits of orange to bright red when the flowers of the following year appear in October and November. Var. *rubra* bearing glowing red-flushed flowers abundantly, fruiting more certainly, makes smaller and more compact growth. Tolerant of lime in the soil, it can be grown in most gardens with rich humus and good drainage.

*A. menziesii* is the Madrona of California and British Columbia. It makes a noble tree up to fifty feet, with smooth bark of cinnamon-red, peeling in flakes with age, large leaves, greyish below, and erect panicles of ivory-white flowers in April and May, followed by roundish, rough orange-red fruits. *A. × andrachnoides* has red-cinnamon bark. These require lime-free, deep, well-drained loams.

Propagate by seeds in February.

# Chokeberry
Family ROSACEAE

*Aronia arbutifolia*

The deciduous shrubs of this North American genus of three species have threefold merit, attractive branching clusters of five-petalled white or pinkish flowers in May, colourful berried fruits, and brilliant foliage colouring in autumn. They are hardy, easily grown, and not particular as to soil.

*A. arbutifolia* makes a shrub of bushy habit, five to eight feet high, with hairy shoots, alternate, ovate, finely toothed leaves of smooth dull green above, grey-haired below; white or pinkish flowers in May followed by small red berries which persist for some time, and brilliant red autumn foliage. *A. prunifolia* (syn. *A. floribunda*) is similar, but flowers in looser clusters, followed by purple-black berries. The Black Chokeberry, *A. melanocarpa*, is a smaller shrub, two to three feet high, and lacks hairiness on its shoots, inflorescence and leaves. Its flowers are white, its berries black, and the autumn foliage turns blushing scarlet.

These shrubs are worth planting for their autumn colour alone, and their low stature makes them suitable for small gardens.

Propagate by seeds in early spring; by cuttings with a heel in late summer; or by division.

**Artemisia**
Family COMPOSITAE

Only a few species of
this large genus which
includes herbaceous
perennials and annual
plants are shrubs.
These are appreciated
chiefly for their attrac-
tive, silver-greyish foliage which gives off a
sweet, fragrant aro-
ma, especially when
crushed. The shrubs
grow easily in any rea-
sonably well-drained
soil, but may only be
truly evergreen in mild
localities.

*Artemisia
abrotanum*

*A. abrotanum*, from
southern Europe, has
various common names
—Southernwood, Lad's Love, Old Man and Old
Woman—throws up erect stems to three feet or so,
is densely clad with feathery foliage of greyish green
leaves, pinnately dissected to fine lobes, and is
highly aromatic. The flowers are dull yellow,
borne in terminal panicles, in September or
October, and of no great distinction. It is more
deciduous than evergreen under British conditions,
and its chief garden merit is foliage contrast. *A.
nutans* of the Canary Islands is silvery-white in
stem and leaf, growing one to three feet, with
pinnately lobed feathery foliage and pale yellow
flowers in crowded leafy panicles in August.

Propagate by cuttings with a heel in July and
August.

41

# Spotted Laurel
Family CORNACEAE

*Aucuba japonica*

The species most representative of this genus and most commonly grown is *A. japonica*, a Japanese evergreen shrub growing six to ten feet tall and with as wide a spread, of rounded, bushy habit, and with large, long oval leaves, leathery glossy on both sides, and on female plants spotted with yellow, and resembling the Laurel. The flowers appear in March or April, small, with four purplish petals in erect terminal panicles, and are unisexual; the male with stamens, the female without. On the female, the pollinated flowers are followed by clusters of bright red oval berries. This shrub will grow under trees and in heavy shade. To be sure of berrying, plants of both sexes must be available. They do well in any ordinary soils.

Many varieties have been raised. Var. *variegata* is a yellow-spotted form; *crassifolia*, male, is esteemed for its thick, broad leaves of deep green; *fructu-albo* and *fructu-luteo* are females with whitish and yellowish berries respectively; *longifolia*, a female with narrow leaves, is perhaps the most free in berrying; *nana rotundifolia* is more dwarf and compact, and berries well, and *viridis* is a fine form with fresh unspotted leaves of glossy green.

Propagate very easily from cuttings in summer.

# Sh
*Berberis*

# Deciduous Barberry
Family BERBERIDACEAE

Some of the most rewarding and easily grown shrubs come from this genus of 450 species, with spring flowers, autumn fruits, and attractive foliage. The leaves alternate and are simple, the stems are armed with spines, usually in threes, the flowers yellowish, and the fruits seeded berries. They thrive in sun or partial shade and in almost any soil which is reasonably well drained.

Most deciduous Barberries are Asiatic in origin, fully hardy, and usually have obovate leaves and red berries.

*Berberis aggregata*

The more notable include: *B. aggregata* (western China), four feet, clustered yellow flowers in July, small red fruits; *B.* × *carminea* (hybrid), four feet, yellow flowers in May, carmine, oval fruits; related forms are 'Fireflame', 'Barbarossa', 'Buccaneer', 'Pirate King', *B. jamesiana* (Yunnan), seven feet, racemes of yellow flowers in May, red berries; *B. thunbergii* (Japan), six feet, flowers with reddish sepals in April, red berries, and its var. *atropurpurea* for foliage colour; *B. wilsonae* (western China), three feet, clustered golden-yellow flowers in May and June, coral-red berries, a parent of many hybrids.

Propagate by cuttings in August or by layering for specimens to type; seeds generally give hybrid plants.

## Evergreen Barberry

Family BERBERIDACEAE

*Berberis*

*Berberis*
*× lologensis*

The evergreen Barberries have leathery leaves, often lance-shaped and toothed, with blue, black or purple fruits. The majority are Asiatic, a few South American. Culture and propagation are the same as for deciduous species.

*B. darwinii* (Chile), eight feet, racemes of orange yellow flowers in April and May, then dark purple fruits, has several forms, and *B. × irwinii* is a related hybrid with dwarf dense habit. What is listed as *B. gagnepainii* is really its var. *lanceifolia* (China), four feet, narrow, holly-like leaves, clusters of bright yellow flowers in May and June, then small, blue-black, egg-shaped fruits. *B. julianae* (China), ten feet, has narrow, spiny-toothed leaves, clustered bright yellow flowers in May, then blue-black oblong fruits; *B. linearifolia* (Chile), four feet, has entire leaves, clustered apricot flowers in May, then blue-black fruits, and a var. 'Jewel', even more striking with red flowers. *B. × lologensis*, a fine hybrid, has fine sprays of apricot flowers in April and May, then oval fruits. *B. × stenophylla*, also hybrid, up to eight feet, has clusters of golden-yellow flowers in profusion in April, then black berries with blue bloom; and many vars. of which *coccinea*, *compacta* and *corallina* are excellent.

The shrubs of the Birch group are chiefly valuable for their pleasing foliage and neat habit. The leaves are alternate and straight-veined; the flowers unisexual, with the female catkins appearing at the end of shoots in spring, and the male being formed in the leaf-axils in autumn to open in spring. The seeds are minute nutlets with a pair of transparent wings.

*Betula nana*

The gem for the shrub garden is *B. nana*, a very hardy native of Britain, Europe and north Asia, slow-growing, of two to four feet in height, with erect branches, finely downy, and circular, round-toothed, short-stalked leaves, a glossy dark green above, attractively net-veined beneath, and small erect female catkins in April. It is happy in any loamy soil, and thoroughly at home in a damp situation. *B. fruticosa* of north-east Asia, and China, grows up to nine feet, and has pleasing oval-shaped leaves, sharply and finely toothed.

Propagation is best done by seeds which only need to be pressed into the soil, without covering, in February or March.

# Butterfly Bush
Family LOGANIACEAE

The beauty of the Buddleias lies in their flowers grouped in rounded panicles or long tapering spikes, attractive to butterflies. The stems are ribbed or angular, the leaves usually opposite, and growth is vigorous in any good loam soil and sunny situation.

The most widely known is *B. davidii*, from western China, growing to fifteen feet, with tapering panicles of orange-eyed flowers and varieties

*Buddleia davidii*

with blue, deep purple, purple-red, white, and pink flowers; var. *nanhoensis*, five to seven feet, is of more dainty and elegant habit. *B. fallowiana*, also Chinese, is deciduous, growing four to eight feet tall, with slender grace, silvery foliage and strongly scented, lavender-blue flower panicles in July; there is a good white var. *alba*. The above species and their varieties benefit by being pruned in late winter. *B. alternifolia*, from China, has the habit of a weeping willow, with alternate leaves, and scented lilac flowers in summer. *B. globosa* is a semi-evergreen from South America, ten to fifteen feet, with wrinkled and netted leaves, and bright yellow, densely packed flowers in three-quarter-of-an-inch balls in June.

Propagate from seeds in early spring, or take late summer cuttings of short side-shoots.

The sparkling green foliage and neat habit of this group of evergreen small trees and shrubs provide background for showier plants in the shrub garden. The leaves grow opposite, leathery and entire, the flowers, beloved by bees, are yellowish-green, without petals, inconspicuous, and unisexual, growing in axillary clusters in April; the stems are squarish. All species are very hardy, succeeding in any

*Buxus*
*sempervirens*

rich soil, particularly chalk, and shaded situations.

*B. microphylla*, Japan, is of neat, rounded shape up to four feet tall, carrying small, bright green leaves, and terminal clusters of small flowers. *B. sempervirens*, the common Box native to Britain, Europe, North Africa and northern Asia, may be grown as a shrub, a clipped specimen or hedge, or small tree of ten to twenty feet. The leaves are ovate, dark glossy green, the flowers pale green with yellow anthers. Of the varieties, *argentea*, leaves with white border, *aureo-variegata*, leaves mottled yellow, and *aurea pendula*, its weeping golden form, *elegantissima*, silver-margined leaves, dwarf-growing, *handsworthiensis*, upright, *prostrata*, horizontal branching or ground cover, and *suffruticosa*, the edging Box, are worthy of note.

Propagate by cuttings with a heel in summer.

# Heather: Ling

Family ERICACEAE

*Calluna*

*Calluna
vulgaris
var. 'H. E.
Beale.'*

The single representative of this genus is *C. vulgaris*, the Heather or Ling; it grows wild throughout northern Europe, Asia Minor and eastern North America. It makes dwarf evergreen bush, up to 24 in. high with dark purple-brown gaunt branches and shoots which are clothed with opposite, minute, scale-like linear leaves, arranged in four rows. The flowers are purplish-pink, with a corolla that persists, and they appear in thin terminal spikes from late June to September. They need a lime-free soil. Acid sands, peaty loams or silts are suitable, with good drainage.

Among the finer forms are: var. *alba*, the White Heather; *alba plena*, with double flowers; *aurea*, one foot, golden foliage; 'County Wicklow', prostrate habit, double pink flowers; 'C. W. Nix', dwarf, bright crimson flowers; *elegantissima*, two feet, soft lilac flowers; *foxii*, very dwarf, pink flowers; 'H. E. Beale', one to one and a half feet, double pink flowers; 'J. H. Hamilton', nine inches, double pink flowers; 'Peter Sparkes', eighteen inches, double pink; 'Robert Chapman', twenty inches, soft purple, foliage changing gold to red; *serlei*, late, white flowers, twenty inches, and vars. *aurea* and *rubra*; 'Sunset', variegated foliage, pink flowers, one foot; and *underwoodii*, mauve to silvery winter buds, ten inches high.

Propagate by cuttings in May. Prune by cutting back hard in spring before growth starts.

**T**
*Camellia*

A genus of handsome evergreen with alternate, simple, toothed, ovate leaves of growing green, and flowers of a showy perfection. Although from tropical or sub-tropical Asia, many species and varieties have proved hardy, though it is best to plant in partial shade, sheltered from the east winds and spring frosts. They like lime-free soil, otherwise good drainage and humus richness suits them well.

*Camellia japonica* var. 'Mme Mandal'

Hardiest is *C. japonica* from Japan and Korea, five to thirty feet, with single flowers of deep scarlet with a boss of yellow stamens, in April to June. There are many forms such as *elegans*, double, carmine rose; 'Gloire de Nantes', semi-double, pink; *magnoliaeflora*, semi-double blush pink; *mathotiana*, double, rose-red; 'Mme. Mandal', and *nobilissima*, double, white.

*C. Sasanqua*, Japan, four to sixteen feet, bears its single white blooms from January, and needs a protecting wall as does *C. saluenensis*, China, with three-inch flowers of white or rose in March. *C. japonica* × *C. saluenensis* are parents of a new race of free-flowering hybrids, such as 'J. C. Williams' 'Mary Christian', pink; 'Donation', semi-double pink; and others.

Propagate from cuttings of nearly ripe wood in August, in a propagating case.

## Trumpet Flower

**Cl Sh**

Family BIGNONIACEAE

*Campsis*

*Campsis radicans*

Two deciduous shrubs climbing by aerial roots and with opposite, pinnate leaves made up of ovate, toothed and pointed leaflets, and large orange-red trumpet-shaped flowers in terminal clusters or panicles, are hardy for the south and south-west, and should be given good loamy soil and a sunny, warm position. The hardier of the two is *C. radicans* (syn. *Tecoma radicans*), the Trumpet Flower of the U.S.A., growing to thirty feet high, clinging by aerial roots, though some support is helpful, with bright green, pinnate leaves, and producing trumpet-shaped flowers, three inches long, one and a half inches wide, of bright orange-red, in terminal clusters of four to twelve, during August and September. The Chinese *C. grandiflora* (syn. *Tecoma chinensis*), grows to twenty feet, but with few aerial roots, and flowers of deep orange and red in panicles of six to twelve, from July to September. Crossing the two species has given hybrids under *C. × tagliabuana* of which 'Madame Galen' with salmon-red flowers is fairly hardy.

Propagate by cuttings in July; by root cuttings in spring. Prune, if needed, in February, cutting back secondary shoots to within a few buds of their base.

# Caryopteris
Family VERBENACEAE

The deciduous shrubs of this genus make a lovely show of colour in late summer with numerous small two-lipped flowers in shades of blue produced freely in branched cymes from the axils and ends of the current season's shoots. The young stems are downy, and the opposite, short-stalked, ovate, often toothed, leaves are a soft dullish green above, grey-white felted below. They like a well-drained sandy loam and a sunny position.

*Caryopteris*
× *clandonensis*

*C. incana* (syn. *C. mastacanthus*), the 'Blue Spiraea' or Moustache plant, of China and Japan, grows three to five feet, leaves are coarsely toothed and flowers violet-blue in rounded axillary clusters in September. *C. mongholica*, Mongolia, is also rather tender, growing two to three feet tall, with linear, entire leaves, downy on both sides, and blue flowers in July and August. Hybrids of the above species, *C.* × *clandonensis*, grows two to four feet, with soft grey-green leaves, and with branching trusses of bright blue flowers from the leaf-axils and ends of shoots in August and September.

Propagate by cuttings taken in May and June, or by seed. Prune annually in spring, cutting back shoots of the previous year's growth to just above suitable buds.

**Cassiope**
Family ERICACEAE

*Cassiope tetragona*

Cassiopes form a group of hardy, low-growing, evergreen shrubs, with minute, opposite, overlapping, scale-like leaves, clinging to the stems in four rows, and solitary, nodding, bell-like flowers in April and May. They are found in alpine or arctic regions, and need a lime-free, moist cold peaty soil, and a situation such as a north aspect, away from bright direct sun.

The tallest species and the most easy to grow is *C. tetragona*, which sends up tufts of erect stems, one foot high, closely packed with the deep-green leaves, and bearing small solitary, white, bell-shaped flowers, nodding on slender stems and sometimes tinged pink. *C. fastigata* of the Himalaya is also uprightish, six to nine inches, the squarish shoots being of closely imbricated green leaves, grooved on the back, and the solitary white flowers being comparatively large. *C. lycopodioides*, from north-east Asia, is just a prostrate mat of squarish leaved, thread-like branches, an inch or so high, with little white bells of flowers in May. *C. mertensiana*, from Alaska, is more erect to ten inches, with white flowers, in April and May; and *C. selaginoides*, from Himalaya, is of tufted erect habit, with white or pinkish flowers.

Propagate by seeds in October, by cuttings in July, by layering in spring.

# Ceanothus
## Family RHAMNACEAE

This genus of some fifty species of shrubs, native to North America, particularly to California, is of special interest for the blueness of its flowers, which, although individually tiny, are numerous in small clusters forming showy spikes or umbels. Some are deciduous, others evergreen. All love the sun, and the evergreens particularly need wall shelter to avoid winter injury. A well drained soil, humus-rich and tending to lightness, is generally suitable.

*Ceanothus*
× 'Gloire de Versailles'

The best hardy deciduous types are hybrids six to eight feet tall, with large, alternate, three-nerved leaves, such as deep blue flowering 'Gloire de Versailles', 'Henri Desfosse', 'Topaz', pink 'Ceres', 'Perle Rose', and 'Marie Simon'. Among the small-leaved evergreens, *C.* × *burkwoodii*, up to eight feet, with oval, glossy leaves and rich blue flowers, July to October, is hardy; but others, *C. dentatus*, four to six feet, rich blue, May, and its var. *impressus*; *C. thyrsiflorus*, to thirty feet, pale blue, May and June, are Californian, and need the shelter of a sunny wall.

Propagate by cuttings in later summer. Prune evergreen wall shrubs immediately after flowering, others in March.

# Leadwort

Family PLUMBAGINACEAE

*Ceratostigma*

*Ceratostigma willmottianum*

The few shrubs of this genus are native to China, with alternate entire leaves that are bristly with forward-facing hairs, and bright blue, five-petalled spreading flowers in terminal heads throughout late summer. The plants are easily grown in light loams, given full sun.

The best type is *C. willmottianum*, making bushy growth two to four feet high, of angled shoots with stalkless, deciduous, diamond-shaped and pointed leaves, and two to three inch wide cluster of bright plumbago-blue flowers from the leaf axils and ends of shoots from the end of July to October. Growth may be killed to ground level in severe winters, but this should be cut away in April, and new growth breaks readily from the base. *C. griffithii* comes from the Himalaya, usually behaves as a deciduous shrub, growing to five feet, with bristly shoots, short-pointed obovate leaves of a dull green with reddish-purple margins and small terminal clusters of bright blue flowers in August and September. It should be given a sunny, hot position against a wall with a soil that is not too rich.

Propagate by cuttings with a heel in July and August or by division in March.

A genus of deciduous trees which are usually low-forking and shrubby under British conditions. Their beauty is two-fold; handsome, alternate, entire rounded and heart-shaped leaves and pea-like flowers in clusters or racemes. Only small young plants transplant well and they should be given a position in full sunshine, in good open soil, and with some shelter from spring frosts.

*Cercis siliquastrum*

The finest species is *C. siliquastrum*, the Judas Tree, from the Mediterranean region, capable of growing to forty feet in native soil, but making a small, bushy tree or spreading shrub of ten to twenty feet in this country. The flowers appear in May before the leaves, clusters of three to six bright rosy purple, pea-like blooms in profusion from young and old branches. The leaves are round and deeply cordate at the base and of glaucous green. *C. canadensis* is the Redbud of central and eastern U.S.A., and is less known for performance, though shrubby in habit when brought into cultivation, with large cordate leaves, and rosy-pink flowers in clusters in May and June. There is a white var. *alba*, and a double *flore pleno*.

Propagation is best attempted by seeds sown under glass in February.

# Japanese Quince

**Sh**

Family ROSACEAE

*Chaenomeles*

*Chaenomeles speciosa*

The species of this genus of deciduous shrubs are now distinguished from *Cydonia* by having toothed leaves and flower styles united at the base. Beautiful for their early flowers, they are fully hardy, easily cultivated and only need full sun and a reasonably good loam soil.

The popular Japanese Quince is now *C. speciosa* (syn. *Cydonia japonica*). It grows from six to nine feet tall, is of dense, spreading habit, and has spiny branches with ovate, alternate, glossy, green leaves. It bears clusters of bright red flowers, one and a half inches across, in March and April, followed by yellowish-green, rounded fruits. Fine varieties include *nivalis*, pure white; and *moerloesii*, rose and white.

*C. japonica* (syn. *Cydonia maulei*) grows low, to three feet, and spreading, with rounded leaves, orange-red flowers, then fragrant yellow fruits; its var. *alpina* is more dwarf with brick-red flowers, and *alba* has white. Crossing above two species has given the hybrid race *C.* × *superba* of which 'Knap Hill Scarlet', large Mandarin red flowers, *simonii*, deep crimson, *alba*, white and *rosea*, pink, are outstanding vars.

Propagate by layering in spring, or by seeds.

# Winter Sweet
Family CALYCANTHACEAE

Only one species of this genus is believed to be in cultivation, the Chinese Winter Sweet, *C. praecox* (syns. *fragrans, Calycanthus praecox* and *Meratia praecox*). It is a deciduous shrub making a bush up to six feet tall, though it is probably most satisfactory grown against a wall.

Its greatest charm lies in the translucent, waxlike, many-petalled flowers, usually facing downward on short stalks from old

*Chimonanthus fragrans*

wood, singly or in pairs, with outer petals of pale yellow, and smaller inner petals stained purple, opening to one inch across on the bare shoots between November and March, and having sweet scent. The foliage is of opposite leaves, ovate and long-pointed, up to seven inches, and a deep lustrous green. Var. *grandiflorus* is more vigorous, producing larger flowers, while the flowers of var. *luteus* are primrose-yellow throughout, sweetly scented, and abundantly produced.

Propagate by layering in May. Prune immediately after flowering in early March, shortening flowered shoots back close to base, and removing all weakly growth. In the open, no pruning is needed. A sunny site and reasonably good loam suit.

# Fringe Tree

**Family OLEACEAE**

*Chionanthus retusa*

The two deciduous shrubs in this group make exceptionally beautiful plants, perfectly hardy, thriving in good loam soil and in open positions. The leaves grow opposite or almost so, and are entire and tapering to the base. The loose panicles of pure white flowers with four narrow petals, are freely produced.

*C. virginica,* the American Fringe Tree, makes a shrub of ten to fifteen feet high, with us, with long, pointed oblong, ovate leaves, and drooping panicles, packed with white flowers having petals an inch long, hanging like a fringe below the branches.

In autumn, the foliage yellows gloriously, and egg-shaped, dark blue berries may appear. The Chinese Fringe Tree, *C. retusa,* grows to ten feet, with smaller ovate leaves, and terminal panicles of the snow-white, strap-like petalled flowers in late June and July, with dark blue berries to follow, under favourable conditions.

It is important to get specimens on their own roots, and not grafted or budded stock, if the plants are to remain robust and in flowering vigour for life. Propagate by seeds.

**Sh**
*Choisya*

# Mexican Orange Blossom
Family RUTACEAE

A genus of one spe-
cies, a most charming
evergreen shrub from
Mexico, *C. ternata*,
which has proved to
have a certain degree
of hardiness for our
gardens, remarkable
in a plant of so warm
a land.

It makes a rounded
bush of six to ten feet,
clothed in opposite,
trifoliolate leaves,
made up of three en-
tire, glossy green,
obovate leaves, taper-
ing to a sessile or al-
most stalkless base,
and giving a strong

*Choisya
ternata*

but unpleasant aroma when crushed. The flowers
are white, five-petalled, and an inch across, and are
borne in clusters of four to six from the leaf-axils
and the ends of shoots, spreading a hawthorn like
scent through the air. The main flowering period
is April and May but intermittent earlier or later
blooming is not infrequent.

While the shrub is hardy enough to survive the
average frosts, it should be given a warm, sunny
position to mature its wood fully, and afforded some
shelter from searing easterly winds which damage
the foliage. It makes an excellent wall shrub, and
its tidy shapeliness makes it a good doorway plant
on the south side of a house. Good drainage and
a light loam suit it perfectly.

Propagate by cuttings of half-ripe shoots in June.

# Rock Rose

**Family** CISTACEAE

*Cistus*

*Cistus*
× 'Silver Pink'

From warm regions of the Mediterranean, this group of evergreen shrubs with opposite, entire leaves and rose-like flowers in May and June, are of dubious hardiness in severe winters. But they flower freely and grow fast and can be kept in being by simple propagation.

The best of the species are *C. crispus*, two to three feet, with wavy-margined, grey downy leaves, and purplish rose flowers; *C. ladaniferus*, the Gum Cistus, three to five feet, with clammy linear-lanceolate leaves, and four-inch single white flowers, blood red at the base; *C. laurifolius*, six to eight feet with white flowers, yellow at the base, of good hardiness. Among the hybrids are *C.* × 'Silver Pink', two and a half feet, silver-grey leaves, and three inch silver-pink flowers; *C.* × *corbariensis*, two to three feet, white flowering; *C.* × *pulverulentus*, two feet, deep rose-pink flowers; *C.* × *cyprius*, six feet, clusters of white flowers, crimson blotched; *C.* × *purpureus*, three feet, large reddish-purple flowers, chocolate blotched at base, and *C.* × *skanbergii*, three to four feet, with pale rose-pink flowers in clusters.

All need a light, sandy soil and full sun. Propagate by cuttings in August.

# Clematis

Family RANUNCULACEAE

*Clematis × jackmanii*

The woody climbing Clematis clamber through and over tall shrubs and trees, as well as up supports placed for them. The leaves are opposite, usually compound, and in the flowers it is the sepals, not the petals, that are showy. All like humus-rich, well drained soil, and do not mind lime. A short list is: *C. armandii*, China, evergreen, to twenty feet, white flowers, April; *C. × jackmanii*, violet-blue flowers summer; 'Comtesse de Bouchard', soft mauvish-pink; *henryi*, white, summer; *C. macropetala*, China, deciduous, blue-flowering, May, June; *C. montana*, Himalaya, grows to twenty-five feet, deciduous, white flowers, May, June; var. *grandiflora* is even finer; 'Lasurstern', deep purplish-blue; 'Nelly Moser', mauve-pink, deep carmine bar; flowering May, June, while 'The President', deep violet, flowers July, October. *C. tangutica*, China, deciduous, ten feet, has rich yellow flowers in July; 'Lady Betty Balfour', rich violet-blue; and 'Ville de Lyon', carmine red, late summer.

Propagate by layering, or cuttings taken July or August.

Prune species that flowers on previous season's growth after flowering; those that bloom on shoots of current growth in February.

## Glory Tree: Glory Bower
Family VERBENACEAE

*Clerodendrum bungei*

Most of the 300 species of *Clerodendrum* (often *Clerodendron*) inhabit hot regions of Africa and the East Indies, and only a few have sufficient hardiness for outdoors in Britain. These are deciduous shrubs or small trees with large, opposite leaves, and the showy clusters of deliciously fragrant flowers that earn the common name of Glory Tree or Glory Bower. They are eligible for favoured gardens which are sunny and warm and well sheltered from east wind and spring frosts, with decent loam soil, freely enriched with peat.

The hardiest is possibly *C. fargesii*, upright and strong-growing to ten feet, with long, ovate leaves, and clusters of starry, white scented flowers in August, followed by porcelain blue berries cradled in persistent crimsoning calyces. *C. bungei* is usually winter-cut to the ground, but sends up a thicket of erect shoots three to four feet with large, toothed, heart-shaped leaves of unpleasant smell when crushed, but the terminal rounded clusters of tightly packed purplish-red flowers appearing in August and September are sweetly fragrant. All come from China.

Propagate by root cuttings in April or by rooted suckers. *C. bungei* can be divided.

**Clethra**
Family CLETHRACEAE

A genus of woody plants, some deciduous, some evergreen, valued for their late summer flowering. The leaves are alternate, toothed and prominently veined, and the flowers are borne in racemes or panicles and are highly scented. They do best in lime-free soils, well-drained, but humus-rich.

*Clethra delavayi*

*C. alnifolia*, the Sweet Pepper-bush of east North America, is a hardy deciduous shrub of upright branching habit to nine feet, with short-pointed, obovate leaves, and erect, spreading sprays of strongly scented white flowers, July to September. *C. tomentosa* of southeast U.S.A., is also a deciduous shrub, eight feet tall, and similar in character, but with very downy young shoots and more spreading flowers. Of the Chinese species, *C. delavayi* is the gem for mild gardens, making an erect, large, deciduous bush or small tree, covered with crowded racemes of cup-shaped white flowers in July and August. *C. barbinervis*, Japan, makes a big bush of beauty, with downy racemes, nine inches long, of very fragrant small white flowers in July and August.

Propagate by layering in spring; by cuttings in July and August, or by seed.

*Colutea arborescens*

This race of deciduous shrubs from southern Europe and the Mediterranean region is colourful and interesting. They have the pinnate, alternate leaves so typical of the Pea family, bear pea-like, yellow or yellowish-red flowers in long-stalked racemes in summer, and large, inflated, bladder-like pods with whitish papery walls in autumn. They are quite hardy, and especially suitable for poor soil.

*C. arborescens* is characteristic of the genus, a vigorous shrub of rounded habit, growing up to twelve feet. The leaves are made up of nine to thirteen oval leaflets, notched at the apex, and the flowers are bright yellow, in clusters from the leaf-axils, from June to October; the bladder-pods are three inches long. *C. orientalis* is of rounded compact habit, growing four to six feet, with grey-green leaves with rounded leaflets, and racemes of coppery-red flowers, followed by one and a half inch pods with open ends. *C. × media*, a hybrid of *C. arborescens × C. orientalis*, has flowers of a bronze or orange-red and, later, three-inch pods.

Propagate from half-ripe shoots in July, or by seeds. Prune in February, cutting forward wood back almost to the base.

**Convolvulus**
Family CONVOLVULACEAE

This genus, although containing some notoriously pernicious weeds, also provides many handsome flowering plants, among them a rather beautiful and striking shrub, *C. cneorum*. This native of southern Europe grows from one and a half to three feet high, and as much across, with branching stems, dressed with evergreen, lanceolate leaves, two inches long, tapering at the base, all covered with silvery-silky hairs, giving a silvery, shin-

*Convolvulus cneorum*

ing, blue-green appearance to the whole plant. The flowers are trumpet-shaped, white or pale pink, hairy on the outside, and are borne in terminal clusters opening successively over a long period from May onwards. It makes a very decorative plant, especially for sunny borders and banks. Its only drawback is that it is only hardy enough for warm gardens in the south, where it should be given a hot sunny spot, and a well drained loam soil which may contain lime or not.

Propagate by cuttings in June in a propagating case.

## Cornel: Dogwood
Family CORNACEAE

*Cornus kousa*

The small trees or shrubs of this genus are deciduous, with opposite, entire, pointed leaves, with well-marked parallel veins, and four-parted flowers. They may be grouped into those with well-bracted flowers, and those without bracts. All grow well in ordinary garden soils.

Of the first group, are *C. kousa*, from Japan, a tree to twenty feet with small, creamy-white bracted flowers in June, and its var. *chinensis* with larger bracts; *C. mas*, the Cornelian Cherry of Europe, a hardy shrub up to fifteen feet, with clusters of yellow flowers in small bracts appearing in February before the leaves, and its golden, and silver variegated vars.; and *C. nuttallii*, western North America, a May-flowering tree of fifteen to twenty-five feet with small flowers, and four to eight creamy-white bracts, flushing pink later. All have autumn foliage colour.

Of the second group, *C. alba*, of Siberia, a spreading shrub to ten feet high, is esteemed for the redness of its stems in winter; var. *atrosanguinea* being more dwarfed and crimson and var. *sphaethii* has finely golden variegated leaves.

Propagate by layering in spring, or by cuttings in summer.

The great charm of the deciduous shrubs of this genus lies in the soft, pure beauty and fragrance of the clear yellow flowers, with bracts at their base, produced in drooping sprays on the leafless shoots in spring. The foliage is of alternate leaves with strong parallel veins, finely toothed, and more or less heart-shaped at the base. All species are hardy and easily grown in

*Corylopsis spicata*

soils that are rich in organic matter and well drained.

*C. pauciflora* from Japan makes a small, rounded shrub with many twiggy branches, three to six feet high, from which dangle open primrose-yellow flowers with creamy-green bracts in clusters of two or three, sweetly scented, in March and April. *C. spicata*, also from Japan, is a spreading shrub, up to six feet, with one-and-a-half-inch-long, drooping sprays of six to twelve yellow, fragrant flowers in March and April, and four-inch-long roundish, cordate leaves later. China gives us *C. sinensis*, a small tree up to twelve feet, with lemon-yellow scented flowers, twelve or more to the spike; *C. platypetala*, a shrub of six feet, with flower spikes two to three inches long; and *C. willmottiae*, up to ten feet, having up to twenty soft yellow flowers per spike.

Propagate by layering in March; by cuttings with a heel in July and August.

# Deciduous Cotoneaster
Family ROSACEAE

*Cotoneaster*

*Cotoneaster salicifolius*

This genus has given us many worthwhile shrubs for our gardens, varying in size, ornamental qualities and attractiveness. They are characterized by somewhat spreading growth, hairy branchlets, entire, stiffish leaves, alternate or in clusters, short-stalked and woolly beneath, small white or pinkish flowers, borne solitary or in clusters, usually in May and June, followed by seed fruits which are often a valuable ornament to the autumn-winter scene.

For hardiness and easy culture, they are hard to excel, and while flourishing at their best in good loams, they also succeed in poor soils, lime or peat.

Of deciduous sorts, *C. bullatus*, western China, six to nine feet, is outstanding for its rugged leaves and brilliant red fruits. *C. horizontalis*, with its fish-bone branches lined with red berries well into the winter, is essential for walls, banks and north aspects. *C. divaricatus*, western China, to six feet, spreads widely, foliage colours finely in autumn, and fruits are scarlet. *C. salicifolius*, China, to twelve feet, is variable, often evergreen with willow-like leaves and red fruits. *C. adpressus*, China, is a prostrate spreading shrub, twelve inches high, of value in clothing banks and rocks.

**Sh**

*Cotoneaster*

# Evergreen Cotoneaster
## Family ROSACEAE

*Cotoneaster franchettii*

Evergreen Cotoneasters add foliage beauty to colourful autumn-berrying habits, and grow easily in most garden soils, and in most aspects.

The best tall growers are the hybrids of *C. frigidus*: *C.* × 'Cornubia', twenty feet or more, with long, lance-shaped leaves, large white flower clusters, yielding to drooping big, bright red fruits; *C.* × *watereri*, a shrub or small tree of twenty feet, with large leaves and masses of large red berries. *C. franchettii*, China, spreads gracefully, eight feet, with small, grey-green leaves, pinkish flower clusters in May and pear-like, orange-scarlet fruits later. From China also comes *C. lacteus*, to twelve feet, long oval leaves milky-grey beneath, and clusters of fine red fruits. *C. simonsii*, Himalaya, not always full evergreen, grows erect to ten feet, carries orange-red berries in autumn. *C. wardii*, Tibet, upright and arching, six to eight feet, with shining small leaves, colouring in autumn, and orange-red fruits, is a fine species. *C. microphyllus*, three feet, but spreading, is good for covering banks; *C. conspicuus*, Tibet, four to five feet, flowers prettily, and is red-berrying. *C. dammeri*, China, is a prostrate carpeter.

Propagate all Cotoneasters by seeds, or by cuttings taken in later summer.

# Hawthorn
Family ROSACEAE

**T**

*Crataegus*

*Crataegus coccinea plena*

The Hawthorn genus is the source of some of the best small trees for gardens. The deciduous leaves are alternate on branches more or less spiny, the flowers usually white and in stalked clusters appearing in May and June, and followed by coloured fruits or 'haws'. The species given here are all hardy, and do well in well-drained loam soils, limed or not, given sunny situations.

*C. monogyna* is the native hedge Hawthorn with deeply lobed foliage; var. *aurea*, the yellow fruiting form is distinctive. The other native *C. oxyacantha*, makes a small tree, fifteen to twenty feet, with two seeds per fruit instead of one. Its best forms are vars. *alba plena*, double white flower, turning pinkish; *coccinea plena*, scarlet flowering; *maskei*, double pale rose flowers; and *rosea*, single pink flowers. *C. prunifolia* is of unknown origin, but the loveliest of thorns, growing to twenty feet, with shining, dark green leaves, abundant June blossom, crimson berries, and richly coloured autumn foliage. *C. pinnatifida* var. *major*, northern China, fifteen to twenty feet, has very large leaves and fine red fruits. *C. × lavallei*, is a notable free-flowering and berrying hybrid, growing to twenty feet.

Propagate by seeds stratified in sand for a year.

**T**
*Crinodendron*

Horticulturally, the plants of this genus of South American evergreen trees have great ornamental appeal, with simple, leathery, deep green leaves, opposite or alternate, and distantly toothed and striking bell- or urn-shaped flowers hanging on long stalks solitary from the leaf-axils. They are only hardy enough to be grown out of doors under the mildest conditions, but thrive easily in a lime-free, humus-rich loam soil in a warm, sheltered spot or at the foot of a south wall, with their roots well shaded from hot sun.

*Crinodendron hookerianum*

The species chiefly grown *C. hookerianum* (syns. *Tricuspidaria lanceolata, C. lanceolatum*) is more simply and happily known as the Chilean Lantern Bush or Tree, growing ten to twenty feet tall, with narrowly lanceolate leaves, five inches long, of dark green, and hanging urn-shaped flowers, three-quarters of an inch long, of a glowing rose-crimson in May and June. It will stand up to pruning or clipping, and can therefore be preserved in shrub or hedge form with dense growth.

Propagate by cuttings of side shoots taken with a heel in July or August, in a propagating frame. Prune or trim in March.

# Broom

Family LEGUMINOSAE

*Cytisus scoparius*
var. *fulgens*

A group of quick-growing, colourful and generally deciduous shrubs. The stems are slender, green and ribbed, with alternate, simple or trifoliolate leaves, pea-shaped flowers, and podded seeds which have a warty appendage characteristic of the genus. They do well in any good well-drained loam soil, love full sun, and do best planted out of pots to avoid root injury.

Dwarf kinds include *C. demissus*, Mediterranean, a brief two to three inches, with yellow, tinged reddish-brown flowers in May and June; *C. decumbens*, from southern Europe, prostrate stems and shining yellow flowers in May and June; *C. ardoinii*, French Alps, six inches, upright branching, with butter-yellow flowers in April and May, and hydrids, *C. × beanii*, one foot, deep yellow flowers, and *C. × kewensis*, one and a half feet, with creamy flowers in May. *C. multiflorus* (syn. *C. albus*) is the white Spanish Broom, upright to ten feet. *C. scoparius*, the common Broom, six feet, is at its best in its vars., *andreanus*, yellow and crimson; 'Cornish Cream', cream; *fulgens*, orange and crimson; 'Firefly', bronze and gold; and 'Golden Sunlight', rich yellow.

Propagate by seeds or summer cuttings.

# Sh
*Daboecia*

# St. Dabeoc's Heath
Family ERICACEAE

This small genus contains two species; neat, evergreen shrubs, with alternate, half-an-inch-long, lanceolate leaves, and egg-shaped flowers in erect, terminal racemes, over a long period. Given a lime-free loam soil, they are easily grown and need little attention.

*Daboecia cantabrica,* var. *alba*

St. Dabeoc's Heath, the Irish and Connemara Heath, botanically *D. cantabrica*, is found in western France, Spain, Portugal and the Azores as well as in Ireland. It makes a dense, compact shrub of one to three feet in height, with recurving, dark glossy green leaves, white felted beneath, and upright racemes, three to six inches long, of large, rose-purple, hanging, egg-shaped flowers from May to September. Var. *alba* is a most charming white-flowering form found in Connemara. Var. *atropurpurea* has flowers of deeper, richer purple than the type. There is a dwarf variety, *nana*, with smaller leaves and smaller flowers. *D. azorica*, from the Azores, is rather less hardy and needs mild conditions, but it makes a low, compact evergreen shrub of four to eight inches, with ruby-crimson flowers in June and July.

Propagate by layers in spring, by cuttings in June to August or by seeds.

# Daphne
Family T<small>HYMELAEACEAE</small>

*Daphne mezereum*

Although providing some of the most beautiful and most sweetly scented of shrubs, the Daphnes are apt to prove capricious to grow. They make small to medium-sized shrubs, with alternate, entire leaves, small flowers with a petal-like, four-lobed calyx, and small, one-seeded berries. They thrive best in humus rich soils which are well-drained and cool. Plant young, leave undisturbed.

The cottage Mezereon, *D. mezereum*, well-known native of Europe, making a globular bush, two to five feet tall, with finely scented, lilac-pink to purplish-red flowers crowding the stems between November and March, before the grey-green leaves appear, is still the best, with red berries later which can be propagated. Var. *alba* is a white-flowering form, and *grandiflora* has larger flowers. *D. cneorum*, the Garland Flower also European, is evergreen, one foot high, with scented, rose-pink flowers in May, and has white var. *alba* and other forms. *D.* × *burkwoodii* 'Somerset', to three feet, flowers bluish-pink, in June.

Propagate by cuttings in summer; species by seeds.

# Desfontainea
Family POTALIACEAE

The genus is one of a single species, *Desfontainea spinosa* (syn. *D. hookeri*), which comes from the Andes of Chile and Peru, sometimes called 'Chilean Holly'.

It makes a magnificent evergreen shrub, capable of growing up to ten feet high, but usually attaining three to six feet in our gardens. The leaves grow opposite, and are very like those of holly, but ovate or oval, and a shining,

*Desfontainea spinosa*

somewhat lighter green, with a spiny edge. The flowers never fail to win admiration, hanging down singly from the shoots, with a funnel-shaped corolla of crimson-scarlet, ending in five yellow tipped, shallow, flared lobes, from a five-parted green calyx, during July to October. A well-drained, loamy soil is suitable, and a position which affords shade, shelter from drying winds, and ample moisture is appreciated. The plant is hardy enough to be grown without much trouble in most gardens in the west, and in places where the moist conditions of its shady native rain forests can be reproduced.

Propagate by seeds, or by shoot cuttings in July or August, rooted in a shaded propagating case or frame.

## Deutzia

Family PHILADELPHACEAE

*Deutzia × rosea*

The genus is one of deciduous shrubs, with brown, peeling bark, thin, opposite, toothed and fine-pointed leaves with minute, star-like hairs on the surfaces, and clusters or panicles of five-parted flowers freely produced in May, June and July. They will grow in quite poor soils, but prefer a good, moist loam with sound drainage, out of the reach of late spring frosts.

Out of some fifty species and many hybrids, some of the best are *D. × magnifica*, a hybrid, six to eight feet tall, with rough leaves, and large, erect clusters of double white flowers in June; *D. × rosea*, a hybrid of compact growth, three feet tall, with frilled, bell-shaped rose-pink flowers in May; var. *grandiflora* being more showy with larger clusters. *D. scabra*, Japan, grows to ten feet with white flowers in big, erect panicles in June and July, and its vars. *candissima* and *plena*, white flushed rose are good. *D. setchuenensis*, three to four feet and its var. *corymbiflora* are fine, late-July, white flowering shrubs; from China.

Propagate by cuttings of half-ripened shoots in July, by division in winter. Prune immediately after flowering or in March.

# Oleaster

Family ELAEAGNACEAE

*Elaeagnus angustifolia*

Attractive foliage, fragrant flowers and handsome fruits mark this group of evergreen and deciduous shrubs, the stems and alternate entire leaves being covered with brown or silvery scales. All are hardy and succeed in ordinary soils, under trees or in shade, and are good for planting in seaside gardens.

Of the deciduous kinds, *E. angustifolia*, the Oleaster of Europe and west Asia grows to fifteen or more feet, with spiny branches, long, narrow, silvery leaves, small yellow scented flowers from the leaf-axils in May, and oval, silver-scaled yellowish edible berries. *E. umbellata*, Himalaya, China and Japan, grows fifteen feet, with silvery-white flowers in May or June, and small red berries. Among the evergreens, *E. macrophylla*, Korea and Japan, makes a rounded, wider shrub, eight to ten feet, with very fragrant, silvery flowers in October. *E. pungens*, Japan, ten to fifteen feet, with wavy-edged leaves and silvery, scented flowers, October, has variegated vars. *maculata*, yellow, *variegata*, cream. *E. × ebbingei* is fast growing to eight feet, and a good windbreak.

Propagate deciduous kinds by seeds, evergreens by cuttings in June and July.

# Chilean Fire Bush

**Sh T**

Family PROTEACEAE

*Embothrium*

*Embothrium coccineum*

This genus of evergreen shrubs or trees from South America can be most fittingly represented by *E. coccineum*, the Chilean Fire Bush or Tree. In Britain it may grow to thirty feet, but as it flowers when only a few feet high, it may also be regarded as a shrub, vividly coloured when in flower. It grows tall, with alternate, lance-shaped or narrowly oval, entire, glossy green, leathery leaves, up to four and a half inches long. The flowers are crimson scarlet, tubular to one and a half inches long, with the four lobes curling back to expose the long erect style. They are carried in racemes of three to four inches long, in the leaf axils and from the ends of shoots, in May and June. It has a var. *longifolium* which comes from the Tierra del Fuego region, with longer and narrower leaves, flowering earlier, and is hardier than the type. Var. *lanceolatum* has narrower leaves still, behaves as a semi-evergreen, and coming from the Andes is reputedly more hardy, and a fine form of it, 'Norquinco Valley Form', collected by H. F. Comber, is now offered. All require a lime-free soil, preferably enriched with peat, and do best in the milder localities such as Cornwall, and possibly North Wales.

Propagate by transplanting of suckers in May.

# Sh
*Enkianthus*

**Enkianthus**
Family ERICACEAE

This group of decidu-
ous shrubs has two
seasons of attraction,
spring, when hanging
clusters of white or
pink bell-shaped
flowers grace the ends
of shoots, and autumn,
when the foliage be-
comes resplendent
in hues of orange and
crimson. The plants
produce their bran-
ches in whorls, with
alternate, ovate and
finely-toothed leaves,
often clustered at the
ends, flowering in
May or June. They
must have a lime-free

*Enkianthus campanulatus*

soil, preferably loamy, and appreciate partial shade.

E. *campanulatus* of Japan is most commonly available, growing slowly from five to eight feet tall, erect and branching, with drooping racemes of creamy yellow, lily-of-the-valley-like flowers, veined and flushed red, and bright red foliage in autumn. E. *cernuus*, also of Japan, is rare but fine, with compact growth up to five feet or so, with small, dark green leaves and tight racemes of white flowers, with frilled petals. E. *perulatus*, Japan, makes slow growth to six feet or more, with dense foliage of oval leaves clustering at the ends of shoots, and clusters of urn-shaped, white flowers in May, followed by glorious autumn colouring of orange and red.

Propagate by layering in June, or by cuttings from June to August.

# Tree Heaths
Family ERICACEAE

*Erica arborea*

The hardy evergreen shrubs of the Heath genus merit representation everywhere. They have small, linear, blunt-ended leaves, usually whorled, and small, egg-shaped, four-parted flowers in shades of white, pink, or purple, profusely produced and lasting long. Most kinds need a lime-free soil, all appreciate good drainage and a soil enriched with leafmould or peat.

*E. arborea*, the Tree Heath, from the Mediterranean, grows to ten feet, with greyish leaves in whorls of three, and sweet-scented, white flowers in terminal clusters in March and April. Only hardy for mild localities, its var. *alpina*, from Spain, is hardier at five to eight feet. *E. australis*, the Spanish Heath, grows four to six feet, with dark green leaves, whorled in fours, and purplish-red flowers in April. The Portuguese Heath, *E. lusitanica*, grows erect and up to ten feet, with pale green leaves, and flowers opening white in March to May. *E.* × *veitchii* is a hybrid, three to six feet tall, with white, scented flowers opening in February. *E. mediterranea*, south-west France and Spain, makes a dense shrub with pink flowers in early spring, three to six feet tall, and has notable vars., such as 'Brightness', bright red flowers; 'W. T. Rackliff', white; *superba*, pink; and *rubra*, red.

# Winter-flowering Heaths

Family ERICACEAE

*Erica carnea*

Winter-flowering heaths are alpine, fully hardy, have a tolerance for lime, and can therefore be grown in any soils which drain well, enriched with peat or leaf-mould. They do well in open situations and as carpeting plants in borders or woodland.

*E. carnea* is the chief species from central and southern Europe. It makes a shrub of six to twelve inches high, and up to eighteen inches spread, with smooth, young stems, carrying linear leaves in whorls of four, and urn-shaped, rose-pink flowers, in one-sided racemes, from December into April. Among the best forms are: 'Queen Mary', rich pink, January and February; 'Winter Beauty', deep pink, November onwards; 'King George', deep pink flowers from November onwards; 'Cecilia M. Beale', a good white with erect habit and early flowering; 'Springwood White', with white flowers and brown anthers showing, and 'Springwood Pink', with pink flowers; *atro-rubra*, dark crimson; 'Ruby Glow', carmine; 'Eileen Porter', pink, and *vivellii*, dark crimson-red with bronzed foliage, are later flowering. *E. × darleyensis*, (*E. carnea × E. mediterranea*) is a rounded shrub of two feet, pale pink from November to April.

*Erica cinerea* var.
'Eden Valley'

Summer and autumn ground colour is provided by heaths which may be found growing wild in Britain.

One is *E. cinerea,* variously known as the Bell, or the Grey, or Scotch Heath, a honey plant for bees on our moorlands and throughout western Europe. It makes a shrub from one to two feet tall, with small, recurved, deep green, linear leaves in threes, and large, rosy-purple, urn-shaped flowers borne in sprays at the ends of shoots, from June to September. A lime-free, humus-rich soil is needed. Of varieties, var. *alba,* nine to twelve inches tall, with long racemes of pure white flowers; 'Apple Blossom', twelve inches tall, with light green leaves and shell-pink flowers; *atrorubens,* ruby-red flowers; 'C. D. Eason', bright red; 'Eden Valley', lilac-pink; 'P. S. Patrick', rich purple; *rosea,* clear, bright pink; are outstanding. *E. ciliaris,* the Dorset Heath, also provides summer and autumn colour, but needs a moist, lime-free soil. It spreads about one foot high, with small, ovate, hairy or fringed leaves, and bright-pink bell-shaped flowers in threes in sprays three to five inches long from July into October. The best white variety is 'Stoborough'; *maweana* with large rose-crimson flowers is commendable.

## Cornish Heath: Cross-leaved Heath
Family ERICACEAE

The Cornish Heath, *E. vagans*, is native to south-west Europe and not reliably hardy. Nevertheless, it adds to the heath colour in summer and autumn, where the soil is lime-free and loamy. It makes a spreading shrub of one to three feet high, with linear leaves in whorls of four or five, and small, purplish-pink flowers from July to November. Var. 'Lyonesse' has clear white flowers with brown anthers; 'Mrs. D. F. Maxwell' has long racemes of warm pink bloom; and 'St. Keverne', rose-pink.

*Erica vagans*

The Cross-leaved Heath, *E. tetralix*, grows in north and west Europe, as well as in Britain, and flowers during June to October. It forms a shrub, six to eighteen inches high, with small, hairy leaves, white below, arranged in fours on the stems, and pink, egg-shaped flowers in terminal clusters. Good vars. are *alba*, white flowering; *mollis*, white hoary foliage, white flowers; 'Pink Glow', pink flowers; and 'Silver Bells', a dwarf with flowers of a lovely silver-pink. *E. × mackayi* (*E. tetralix × E. ciliaris*) is dwarf with bright pink flowers, and has vars. 'Dawn', deep rose, and 'H. Maxwell', rose-red, of merit.

All the Ericas are easily propagated by cuttings in June to August, rooting freely in peaty soils.

# Chilean Gum Box

**Sh**

Family ESCALLONIACEAE

*Escallonia*

*Escallonia × edinensis*

This genus of evergreen shrubs hailing from South America, chiefly Chile provides many valuable subjects for planting in seaside and windy gardens in mild western localities, and for floral beauty on walls, but discrimination is needed, especially for inland and northern gardens, as hardiness is often suspect. Growth is erect and branching, with finely-toothed alternate leaves, with short or no stalks, and small flowers, five-parted, in terminal panicles or racemes. They will grow in all ordinary garden soils, and like sun.

Of the species, *E. macrantha*, from Chile, growing six to ten feet, densely foliaged with large, shining deep green, toothed leaves, and rose-crimson flowers from June to September, is good for hedges and walls. *E. virgata*, deciduous, lime-intolerant, and hardy, has white flowers, June to August. There are many beautiful hybrids of varied parentage also, of which some notable forms are: 'Apple Blossom', pink and white; 'C. F. Ball', crimson; 'Donard Beauty', rosy-red; 'Donard Brilliance', crimson; × *edinensis*, neat, four feet, rose-pink; × *langleyensis*, rose-crimson; × *exoniensis*, white; and × *iveyi*, tall white.

Propagate by cuttings in late summer in a propagating case.

**Brush Bush**
Family EUCRYPHIACEAE

Distinctive in habit and foliage, the shrubs of this genus are evergreen or nearly so, with opposite leaves, and bear white, four-petalled flowers, opening like single roses, with a thick brush of anthers. They are somewhat slow coming into flower and tender when young. They are best suited to mild localities of the south-west in the open, and for sheltered walls elsewhere.

*Eucryphia glutinosa*

The hardiest is *E. glutinosa* of Chile, making an upright, branching shrub to fifteen feet, with shining green, pinnate leaves of three or five oval, toothed leaflets, colouring yellowish in autumn, and two-and-a-half-inch white flowers at the ends of shoots in August. It needs a lime-free, well-drained, cool soil. Another Chilean, *E. cordifolia*, may grow to forty feet, with stiff, dark green, narrow heart-shaped leaves, and clear white flowers in August. Hybrids are *E.* × 'Nymansay', erect, evergreen, and tree-like to thirty feet, with yellow-anthered, white flowers, and *E.* × 'Rostrevor', also evergreen and tree-like to thirty-five feet, with two-inch white flowers in August. All but *E. glutinosa* will grow in free-draining loam soal, and do not object to chalk or lime.

Propagate by layers in spring or by cuttings in June.

# Euonymus

Family CELASTRACEAE

*Euonymus japonicus* var. *aureus*

The genus contains widely different shrubs or small trees, opposite, finely-toothed leaves, small flowers in axillary clusters and pendulous fruits, lobed or winged, and brightly coloured. The species given here are hardy, and can be grown in almost any soil.

Of the deciduous sorts, *E. alatus*, the Winged Spindle Tree of China and Japan, is a shrub, slow-growing to six feet, with branches having two thin corky wings, oval, dark-green leaves, yellowish June flowers, and lobed purplish fruits, with fine rosy-crimson autumn foliage. *E. europaeus*, the Common Spindle Tree, makes a shrub or tree up to twenty feet, attractive for its red lobed fruits with orange-coated seeds. *E. latifolius*, Europe, ten to twenty feet, is spreading, with rosy-red fruits and rich red autumn leaves. *E. sachalinensis*, ten feet, and *E. yedoensis*, twelve feet, are fine autumn colouring species with reddish fruits from Japan. *E. japonicus*, Japan, with oval, evergreen leaves, is used for hedges or as a shrub, up to ten feet or more, and has many forms, golden-silver-variegated and pyramidal. *E. fortunei* v. *radicans*, Japan, is a trailing evergreen for ground cover or walls, and has several related lovely variegated varieties.

Propagate deciduous species by seeds in February, evergreens by cuttings in May and June.

**False Heath**

*Fabiana*

Family SOLANACEAE

Two charming evergreen species of this South American genus have entered our gardens from Chile. Although heath-like in appearance, with erect and spreading, tapering, downy branches, having numerous short, slender twigs, crowded with alternate, tiny, stiff, scale-like, triangular leaves, and terminating in erect tubular flowers in June, the shrubs are more closely related to the Nightshade and Potato. They are not fully hardy, and are therefore only eligible for the open in mild and sheltered gardens, where they thrive in a well-drained, light soil, acid or limy, and abundant sunshine.

*Fabiana imbricata*

F. *imbricata* grows erect and may attain a height of three to six feet. Its branches become heath-like plumes when bearing the white, erect tubular flowers in June. There is a dwarf form, var. *prostrata*, with pale mauve flowers with a reputation of greater hardiness. F. *violacea* is a shrub of similar habit to F. *imbricata*, but grows more quickly and not so tall, with flowers that vary in colour from milk-blue to a washy mauve. It is less striking, but reputedly more hardy.

Propagate by cuttings with a heel in late summer. Prune after flowering, if necessary.

# Fatsia
Family ARALIACEAE

*Fatsia japonica*

The genus is one of two species, notable for their large handsome, evergreen leaves, growing alternate on thick stems, and bearing large panicles of white flowers late in the year.

The better known is *F. japonica* (syn. *Aralia sieboldii*), often grown as an indoor or greenhouse plant. It is, however, reasonably hardy and can be grown out of doors where it is given a sheltered and fairly well shaded position, and freedraining, loamy soil, and is excellent for seaside planting in the south-west, where it will stand up to the sea winds. This Japanese evergreen gives a bold and tropical look to gardens, well suited to terraces, courtyards and formal surroundings. It grows eight to twelve feet tall, with thickish stems, long, leathery, shining green leaves, palmately lobed, particularly striking when young and unfolding, and branching panicles of milky-white flowers in October. The Chinese *F. papyrifera*, with pithy shoots, and flowers in panicles up to thirty inches long at the ends in October, needs the warmth of a sheltered Cornish garden.

Propagate by cuttings with a heel in August.

**Sh**

*Forsythia*

*Forsythia × intermedia* var. *spectabilis*

There are six species in this genus of beautiful, easily grown, spring-flowering, deciduous shrubs. The shoots are four-angled, with opposite, simple or trifoliolate leaves, ovate and roughly toothed in outer half, and the yellow flowers burst from lateral buds on wood of the previous year's growth before the leaves unfold. All are hardy, grow in various aspects and in any reasonably well-drained soil.

*F. ovata*, Korea, a compact shrub of three to four feet, and slow-growing, bears golden-yellow flowers in March. *F. suspensa*, China, spreads wide and tall, to ten feet, with golden-yellow flowers in March and April, var. *fortunei* is good. *F. viridissima*, east China, grows stiffly erect to six or eight feet, with large, bright yellow flowers in April. Crossed with *F. suspensa*, the last has given us *F. × intermedia*, graceful and robust to ten feet tall, with yellow flowers in March of which forms 'Beatrix Farrand', 'Lynwood', *primulina* and *spectabilis*, are very fine.

Propagate by softwood cuttings taken in July, or cuttings taken with a heel in October. Little or no pruning should be necessary, but if done, cut immediately flowering is over.

89

*Fothergilla monticola*

The genus belongs to the south-eastern states of North America; deciduous shrubs of good habit, with alternate, stalked, obovate leaves, coarsely toothed and flowers without petals but with many, long, conspicuous stamens with white thickened tops, crowded in erect, bottle-brush-like heads appearing before the leaves, and being attractively ornamental. In autumn the leaves turn crimson or orange and pay another dividend of beauty. The shrubs are hardy, but do best in a sandy-peat loam of good drainage and some shade.

*F. major* is a shrub of six feet or so, with feathery white spikes of fragrant flowers in April, and the foliage colours a rich orange-yellow in autumn. *F. gardeni* (syn. *alnifolia*) makes a small shrub two to four feet tall, with sweet-scented spikes of white-stamened flowers in April and May, and small, leaves, colouring crimson in autumn; *F. monticola* grows three to five feet high, with milk-white flower-brushes in April, and leaves that crimson in the autumn.

Propagate by cuttings taken with a heel in summer, or by seeds in February, though slow-germinating. No regular pruning is needed.

## Sh

*Fuchsia*

# Fuchsia
## Family ONAGRACEAE

None of the hundred species of this genus are fully hardy for our gardens. They come from Central and South America and New Zealand, and are killed to ground-level in our winter, but some species send up new shoots readily from the base each year, and their fresh green, opposite or whorled leaves, and exotic drooping flowers with long protruding stamens are most welcome for summer and autumn colour. They succeed in any decent loam, welcome partial shade, and do not mind woodland conditions. A covering of

*Fuchsia magellanica*

leafmould or peat and soil over the crown of the plants ensures survival.

The hardiest plants are *F. magellanica* of southern South America. The type may grow to six feet or more, with bright green, ovate, toothed leaves, and nodding flowers made up of a red tube and four spreading red sepals, purple to blue petals, and eight stamens, June to October, and vars. *riccartonii*, four to eight feet, very hardy, free-flowering, red and purple; 'Madame Cornelissen', red sepals, white cupped flower; 'Mrs. Popple', larger flowers. There are also many choice named garden hybrids.

Propagate by cuttings in summer. Prune in spring.

## Silver Tassel Bush
Family GARRYACEAE

*Garrya*

*Garrya elliptica*

A group of evergreen shrubs which have ornamental garden value, partly in their foliage made up of opposite, entire, ovate leaves, wavy-margined and dark green with greyish down beneath, but chiefly for their silvery-grey catkins which are made up of small, insignificant flowers within cup-shaped bracts and are unisexual. The shrubs grow freely in any ordinary garden soil, but deserve some shelter from chilling winds and foliage-spoiling frosts. They resent root disturbance and are best planted out of pots, when young, in permanent quarters, preferably on a slope to the south or west, or a sunny wall facing these quarters, with protection against north and east winds.

The hardiest species is *G. elliptica*, from California and Oregon, growing to six to twelve feet, with oval to roundish leaves, and silver-grey flowering tassels hanging clustered at the ends of shoots, three to six inches long, and often longer on male plants in mild quarters, while on female trees the catkins are shorter but may hang from November into February.

Propagate by half-ripened cuttings in August. Prune immediately after flowering, if necessary.

# Gaultheria
Family ERICAEAE

The hardy evergreen shrubs of this genus have much ornamental beauty in their foliage of leathery, alternate leaves, their bell- or urn-shaped flowers, and their berry-like capsular fruits. They need a lime-free soil, preferably humus-rich and well-drained, and appreciate partial shade, or grow in full shade.

*Gaultheria cuneata*

*G. procumbens* is the Canada Tea, Creeping Wintergreen, Checkerberry or Partridge Berry of North America, a creeping shrub with shoots to six inches high, clustered with small, finely-toothed, ovate leaves to the top, and with solitary, white flushed pink flowers from the leaf-axils in July and August, followed by bright red, rounded fruits. Other creepers are *G. cuneata*, western China, a compact shrub of one foot or so, white-flowering in June, and white-berried later; *G. shallon*, the North American Salal, makes a dense bush, two to four feet tall, with large, dark green leaves, pale pink bell-flowers in May and June, and purple-black fruits. *G. hookeri*, Himalaya, may grow to six feet, bears pink flowers in April, and needs a sheltered site.

Propagate by cuttings taken in August, or by seeds.

# Genista

Family LEGUMINOSAE

*Genista*

*Genista hispanica*

Like *Cytisus*, a closely related genus, this group of deciduous shrubs is commonly called Broom. The fresh green stems furnished with alternate leaves, and the pea-like flowers, are borne in terminal racemes, giving way to small, linear pods. The species given do well in light, well-drained soils and sunny positions, and are best planted out of pots and left undisturbed.

Tallest are *G. aethnensis*, the Mount Etna Broom, ten to fifteen feet, of Sicily, with masses of golden July flowers; and *G. tenera* (*G. virgata*), the Madeira Broom, upright to six to twelve feet, and short, terminal racemes of yellow flowers in June and July. *G. cinerea*, south-west Europe, grows three to nine feet, with yellow flowers from July to September. The Spanish Gorse, *G. hispanica*, makes a neat but spiny shrub of two to three feet, with golden-yellow flowers in May and June; the Dyer's Greenweed, *G. tinctoria*, of Britain and Europe, one to three feet, is best in its double var. *flore pleno*, spreading low, with double yellow flowers in June. *G. lydia*, Balkans, eighteen inches high, is excellent with butter-yellow bloom in June.

Propagate by seeds in early spring, by cuttings in summer.

**T**
*Halesia*

## Silver Bell: Snowdrop Tree
Family STYRACACEAE

The North American species in this genus make beautiful, small ornamental trees. They are deciduous with fairly large, ovate-oblong, pointed, and slightly toothed alternate leaves, showy, white, four-petalled, pendent clustered flowers rather like snowdrops on the wood of the past year, in May and June; followed by four-winged seeded fruits later. They are hardy, but are best given a spot sheltered from chilling east winds and spring frosts in the interests of the blossom, and appreciate well-drained, deep, light loams free of lime.

*Halesia carolina*

*H. carolina* (syn. *H. tetraptera*), south-eastern U.S.A., makes a low branching tree or large shrub of fifteen to twenty-five feet, with spreading branches, draped with clusters of five or six white, snowdrop bell flowers a little before the long, ovate, slender-pointed leaves unfold in May. *H. monticola*, central U.S.A., is the Mountain Snowdrop Tree, making a shapely tree of thirty feet, with larger flowers than those of *H. carolina*, appearing with the leaves in late May, and beginning to flower while quite young. It has a var. *rosea* with flowers flushed a pale rose-pink.

Propagate by layering or by root cuttings in April. No regular pruning is needed.

# Halimium
Family CISTACEAE

*Halimium ocymoides*

The small evergreen shrubs of this genus form a group very closely related to *Helianthemum*, with opposite, entire leaves, but differing in flower structure in that the style is quite short and straight instead of long and curved. Halimiums are native to the Mediterranean region and therefore need sunny, warm positions, and well-drained soils, doing well where there is lime. They may suffer injury in severe winters unless protected.

*H. lasianthum formosum*, the Sweet Cistin from Portugal, is perhaps the hardiest species, slow-growing, spreading shrub, two to three feet high, with grey downy stems, small oblong leaves, and golden-yellow flowers, stained chocolate near the base of the petals, two inches across, in June and July. Another fine Portuguese species is *H. ocymoides*, dense and bushy with downy-grey leaves, and panicles of bright-yellow flowers purple-brown at the base of each petal, in June and July, one and a half to two and a half feet tall. *H. umbellatum* grows erect to eighteen inches, with white flowers, yellow-centred, in erect clusters in June.

Propagate by cuttings taken in June. Any pruning should be done after flowering, but it is better to layer the shoots.

# Witch Hazel

Family HAMAMELIDACEAE

*Hamamelis mollis*

The glory of the Witch Hazels, a group of deciduous shrubs, lies in their flowers which appear on the bare twigs in winter and consist of four narrow, ribbon-like petals, out of a four-sepalled calyx, often coloured within. The leaves alternate and hazel-like and may colour a pleasing yellow in autumn. They are hardy, and at their best in well-drained, humus-rich acid loams, and appreciate dressings of peat or leafmould; in sunshine or partial shade.

The Chinese Witch Hazel, *H. mollis*, seven to ten feet tall, is reputed the best, with deep golden-yellow, scented flowers in January and February, and lemon-yellows on var. *pallida*. In the Japanese Witch Hazel, *H. japonica*, growth is spreading up to eight feet, and the flowers have crumpled yellow petals, with purplish calyces; var. *arborea*, growing to twenty feet, golden-yellow flowers; *zuccariniana* is similar but the flowers are lemon-yellow. Their hybrid, *H.* × *intermedia*, has provided colourful forms in 'Carmine Red', 'Diane', 'Jelena' and 'Moonlight'.

Propagate by seeds, germination taking two years; by grafting on seedlings of *H. virginiana* in March and April.

# Shrubby Speedwell

**Sh**

Family SCROPHULARICEAE    *Hebe* (syn. *Veronica*)

*Hebe* (syn. *Veronica*) *hulkeana*

The Shrubby Speed-wells, eligible for our gardens, are chiefly native to New Zealand. They are ever-green, with opposite, entire leaves in four distinct rows, and carry axillary or ter-minal spikes of small, four-parted flowers in the latter half of summer. Many are tender, and those given here welcome a well-drained loam soil, sunny positions and warm maritime or well-sheltered gar-dens where frosts are unlikely to be troublesome.

For hardiness, the most valuable are *H. brachy-siphon*, bushy and rounded to six feet, small leaves, hidden by two-inch racemes of white flowers in July; *H. andersonii*, erect, three feet spikes of violet flowers in autumn; and *H. hectori*, rigid stout shoots, with scale leaves, one to three feet, white or pinkish flowers in July. For floral beauty under mild conditions, *H. hulkeana*, two to six feet, with lavender-blue sprays in May and June; *H. lyallii*, eighteen inches, white and rose flowers in June; *H. pagei* one to three feet, white flowers from June to August; and *H. speciosa*, four to five feet, and its hybrids with flowers of blues, red, and purples, are all worthy of careful consideration.

Propagate by softwood cuttings from May to July in a propagating case or frame.

# Sh

*Helianthemum*

*Helianthemum vulgare*

The shrub species are delightful for the front of shrub borders and rock gardens, given full sun. The leaves are small, entire and opposite, and the five-parted flowers, opening flat like single roses, are freely borne in terminal racemes throughout June and July. They are hardy, and do best in well-drained light soils and revel on limestone and chalk.

The common Sun Rose, *H. nummularium* (syn. *H. chamaecistus*), of south-east Europe, growing to six to eighteen inches high and spreading to two feet or more, has a host of colourful varieties such as 'Ben Heckla', brick red; 'Ben Adler', orange-red; 'Ben Dearg', crimson lake; 'The Bride', white, and 'Wisley Primrose', primrose yellow; also double-flowering sorts such as 'Jubilee', straw yellow; 'Mrs. Earle', red; 'Rose of Leewood', pink; and 'Watland's Red', deep red. *H. alpestre*, southern Europe, is a charming dwarf of four inches, with small yellow flowers. *H. apenninum*, Europe, spreads low, eighteen inches high, with white flowers; it has a rosy-red var. *roseum*.

Propagate by softwood cuttings in June. Prune after flowering.

*Hibiscus
syriacus*

This genus may be handsomely represented in the shrub garden by *H. syriacus*, the Bush Mallow or Bush Hollyhock, introduced from India and China late in the sixteenth century. It is hardy, deciduous, and a late-flowering shrub, growing slowly to eight feet, with upright habit, having greyish bark, alternate, slender-stalked leaves, three to four inches long, generally ovate, but three-lobed and coarsely toothed. The flowers appear singly in the leaf-axils of young shoots, and are hollyhock-like, trumpet-shaped, and up to four inches across, during autumn. The plants grow readily in most soils and deserve a sunny position, doing best under dry climatic conditions.

There are many varieties, and among the best are: var. *coelestis*, single, deep blue flowers; 'Hamabo', single, pale bluish-pink with crimson centre, late flowers; 'Snowdrift', single, white; and 'Woodbridge', which has very large, single flowers of a rich rose-pink, blotched maroon in the centre.

Propagate by cuttings taken with a heel, under a handlight, in July. No regular pruning needed, but may be spurred, by shortening lateral shoots after flowering.

## Sh
*Hippophae*

*Hippophae rhamnoides*

The two species of this genus make tall deciduous shrubs or trees, with branching habit, the shoots often spine-tipped, and alternate, linear leaves, three inches long, dark green above, silvery below, and small, rather insignificant flowers in axillary clusters, on the old wood in April. The sexes are separate and to secure the clusters of brilliant orange-yellow berries, at least one male plant should be set among six to eight females. The plants are hardy, and will grow in any ordinary soil, and are especially useful in maritime districts for windbreaks.

*H. rhamnoides*, the Sea Buckthorn, will grow up to forty feet, but can be kept within bounds by pruning. The silvery-grey young shoots and linear leaves are attractive, but the real beauty of the shrub lies in the small, round, shiny, orange-yellow fruits which cluster the branches in autumn, and being disliked by birds, persist well into the winter. The shrub is a native of temperate Europe and Asia. *H. salicifolia*, comes from the Himalaya with pale yellow fruits, less freely produced.

Propagate female plants by layering in May; for hedges, plants can be raised from seeds in spring. No regular pruning required.

*Hydrangea macrophylla* var. 'Europa'

This group of shrubs is supreme for midsummer to autumn floral colour; deciduous, with leaves opposite, and flowers in terminal panicles or clusters, the outer flowers often bracted and sterile. They are hardy, and thrive in any good, well-drained, humus-rich loam, pink flowering on soils containing lime, blue on acid. The addition of aluminium sulphate fosters blueness. They grow best in partial shade and deserve shelter.

*H. macrophylla* the Mophead, from Japan, four to eight feet, has many forms—white: 'Mme. E. Mouillière'; pink: 'Parsifal', 'Europa', and 'Hamburg'; red: 'Westfalen', 'Maréchal Foch', and 'Vulcain'; and blue (from pink): 'Vicomtesse de Vibraye', 'Kluis superba', and 'Altona'. 'Lanarth White', 'Blue Wave' and *lilacina* are 'Lacecap' varieties, with large flowers surrounding scented small ones. Of other species, *H. paniculata* var. *grandiflora*, six to nine feet, Japan, with pointed panicles of white turning pink flowers; *H. serrata*, four feet, from Japan, with white, blue and pink varieties, and *H. villosa*, eight feet, China, blue-flowered, are worth planting.

Propagate by cuttings of half-ripened leafy shoots in July and August. Prune and thin in February.

**St. John's Wort**
Family GUTTIFERAE

This large genus provides many shrubs notable for their long and generous show of beautiful, five-petalled, stamen-bristling yellow flowers from spring till autumn. The leaves grow opposite or in whorls, marked with transparent glands. The species noted here are hardy, easily cultivated in any reasonably good, well-drained loam and in sunny positions.

*Hypericum calycinum*

One of the hardiest is *H. calycinum*, the 'Rose of Sharon' from the Orient, one foot high, but spreading vigorously, even under trees, with large lemon-yellow flowers, June to September. Growing upright to four feet or more, 'Rowallane Hybrid' (*H. hookerianum rogersii × H. leschenaultii*) is large flowering. *H. patulum*, an evergreen from China, growing to three feet, with bushy habit, is best represented by var. 'Hidcote' with the largest of flowers.

A good dwarf of one to one and a half feet, is *H. × moserianum* (*H. × calycinum × H. patulum*), with ovate, grey-green leaves, and dense terminal clusters of small yellow flowers; its var. *tricolor* has flowers marked with white edged with red.

Propagate by cuttings in June, by rooted runners, by seeds in early spring. Prune, if desired, in February.

# Holly

Family AQUIFOLIACEAE

*Ilex aquifolium*

The hardy hollies give us beauty in foliage and fruit. The leaves are alternate, often toothed but may be entire. The flowers are small, whitish, appearing in spring or early summer. As the plants are unisexual, only females berry. They do well in any good well-drained loam, in sun or shade, and stand up to wind quite well. *I. aquifolium* is the evergreen, common Holly of Britain, Europe and Asia, making a tree of sixty feet, with dark glossy green, spiny-toothed leaves, and bright red berries on the female form in autumn and winter. Of the varieties, fine males for foliage are 'Silver Queen' and 'Golden Queen'. The best of the female berrying kinds include: *fructu luteo*, yellow-berrying; 'Golden King', golden-bordered leaves; and *pyramidalis*. A mixture of males and females is needed for effective berrying. *I. cornuta*, China, densely evergreen bush to eight feet, has large oblong, spined leaves, and *I. crenata*, Japan, five to ten feet, small, lance-shaped leaves; *I. pernyi*, China, five to ten feet, has distinctive, long-spined foliage and berries freely.

Propagate by seeds, stratified in sand for a year, by cuttings in August under handlight. Prune in April or September.

# Indigofera
Family LEGUMINOSAE

The few hardy species of this group of deciduous, leguminous shrubs are attractive with elegant, alternate, pinnate leaves, and racemes of broom-like, pink or purple flowers, freely produced from the leaf-axils of growing shoots successively through summer and autumn. They do best in open, well-drained loams, and should be given warm, sunny positions.

*Indigofera decora*

*I. gerardiana*, Himalaya, is reasonably hardy, growing three to four feet, with graceful, spreading habit in the open, taller on walls, having light, green-grey foliage made up of pinnate leaves, and flowers of bright purplish-rose in racemes up to five inches long, from June onwards. *I. hebepetala*, also from the Himalaya, grows to four feet, with long racemes of rose flowers, with a deep crimson standard. Other attractive kinds from China include *I. pendula*, arching and spreading, with leaves to ten inches, from stems reaching five to eight feet tall; and *I. potaninii*, four to six feet, with flowers of clear pink in racemes of three to five inches.

Propagate by cuttings taken with a heel in June. Prune in February, cutting hard back.

Family OLEACEAE

*Jasminum*

*Jasminum nudiflorum*

This is a variable genus of upright, climbing or trailing shrubs with several hardy species that are easily grown in any reasonably good garden loam, such as the fine winter-flowering *J. nudiflorum* from China, its green stems ornamented with scented, yellow flowers, springing singly from axils from November onwards. It is best against a wall, growing twelve to fifteen feet high. The Common Jasmine, *J. officinale*, Persia, ten feet, is best trained on a wall, where its deciduous, pinnate, opposite leaves, and a terminal cluster of fragrant white flowers, can be best displayed in June to September. *J. beesianum*, China, makes rather tangled rose-pink flowers in ones to threes in June and July; but its hybrid with *J. officinale*, *J. × stephanense*, grows to fifteen feet, *J. parkeri*, north-west India, twelve inches, with small, alternate, pinnate leaves, yellow flowers in June and *J. revolutum*, Himalaya, a spreading shrub to eight feet, with terminal clusters of six to twelve yellow flowers in July and August are well worth planting.

Propagate by cuttings of half-ripened shoots in August. Prune after flowering.

*Kalmia latifolia*

Anyone who gardens on a lime-free, friable, well-drained, but humus-rich loam and in a mild locality should find room for one of the evergreen shrubs of this group. The leaves are entire, oval or lanceolate and crowded radially at the ends of shoots, but the full beauty lies in the cup-shaped flowers borne in clusters in late spring or early summer, followed by egg-shaped seed capsules. They like sunshine tempered by the open branches of nearby shrubs in the hot summer months.

*K. latifolia*, the Mountain Laurel or Calico Bush of eastern North America, grows bushy, three to eight feet tall, with alternate, glossy green, lance-shaped leaves, and large clusters of many saucer-shaped, shell-pink flowers from the wood of the previous year in June and July. Var. *myrtifolia* is an excellent low form, two to three feet tall, dense with small-leafed foliage and flowers of a deeper pink. *K. polifolia* (syn. *K. glauca*), U.S.A., is dwarf and spreading, with narrow, bright green leaves, and rosy-purple flowers in terminal clusters, in April and May; var. *microphylla* is a delightful dwarf of six inches, with pretty rose-lilac flowers.

Propagate by layering in May; by cuttings in August.

# Jew's Mallow
Family ROSACEAE

*Kerria japonica*

The single species that represents this genus has been in cultivation with us for over two hundred years, and is an old, much-admired subject in cottage gardens. It is *K. japonica*, originally from China, a deciduous shrub that throws up erect, slender green shoots to four or six feet, branching into zigzagging, twiggy branchlets with a leaf at each corner. The foliage is freshly green, the alternate leaves being long-pointed, ovate, with heart-shaped base and sharply double-toothed margins. The flowers are a buttercup-yellow, appearing singly at the end of lateral shoots, with a single row of five petals, in April and May. It makes an elegant plant for the border or a wall. It var. *flore pleno*, which grows taller, more erect and more robustly, is a good wall plant, carrying numerous orange-yellow, double, ball-shaped flowers, up to two inches across, from April to June or longer. Kerrias are easy to grow, doing well in any good, reasonably well-drained garden soil, even chalk, and in sun or partial shade.

Propagate by division in March; by layering in May; by cuttings of young shoots in June and July, under handlights. Prune immediately after flowering, thinning the older wood.

# T
*Koelreuteria*

*Koelreuteria paniculata*

The genus is one of highly attractive, small, deciduous trees coming from east Asia. *K. paniculata*, variously known as the China Tree, the Golden Rain Tree, and Pride of India, is best known, being introduced from northern China in the eighteenth century. It is a pity it is not planted more, for it is reasonably hardy, of very graceful and interesting habit, and makes a fine specimen tree of fifteen to thirty or forty feet tall. It grows well in any good, well-drained, loam soil, and flowers freely when given a sunny, sheltered site. The foliage is unusual in that the leaves are usually pinnate or double-pinnate, with alternate leaflets which are ovate, but unevenly notched and toothed and one to two inches long. In July and August, when their brightening colour is highly welcome, large, many-flowered panicles of small yellow flowers break out at the ends of shoots, followed by inflated, two-inch fruits with papery tri-lobed walls, containing three seeds. In autumn the foliage turns to a bright yellow.

Propagate by seeds in early spring, by root cuttings in May, by cuttings of young shoots under a handlight in August. No regular pruning is needed.

*Kolkwitzia
amabilis*

The genus embraces only one species, a deciduous shrub of considerable charm, *K. amabilis*, sometimes called 'Wilson's Beauty Bush' after E. H. Wilson, who collected it in the Hupeh province of China and introduced it at the beginning of the present century. It is a deciduous shrub of erect habit, growing three to six feet tall, with rough or bristly stems, clothed with broad ovate, deeply veined, hairy and short-stalked leaves, distantly toothed and ending in a long, recurving point, growing opposite. The flowers are freely produced in late May and June, being half an inch long, bell or funnel-shaped with the mouth five-lobed, and beautifully coloured pink with yellow throat, in corymbs up to three inches across, borne at the ends of lateral branchlets. The shrub is hardy and will grow well in any good garden soil which drains well and contains humus, and does best in a sunny, hot position, with the roots mulched.

Propagate by two- to three-inch-long cuttings of the current year's shoots, inserted in a propagating case or frame in June or July. The only pruning needed is an occasional thinning of the stems after flowering.

**Sh T**
*Laburnum*

**Golden Chain**
Family LEGUMINOSAE

The genus is one of deciduous trees with alternate, long-stalked trifoliolate leaves, and drooping racemes of small pea-like yellow flowers. Perfectly hardy, thriving in almost any garden soil and position, they are easily grown.

The Common Laburnum or Golden Chain, *L. anagyroides*, from southern Europe, grows to twenty feet, with grey-green, downy leaves, and pendulous racemes of golden-yellow flowers followed by small pods of black seeds which are poisonous. There is a striking golden-leafed var. *aureum*. The

*Laburnum anagyroides*

Scotch Laburnum, *L. alpinum*, from south-east Europe, grows more compact with longer, narrower racemes of yellow flowers in June. Crossed with *L. anagyroides* it gives hybrids, *L.* × *vossii* and *L.* × *watereri*, which have very long flower racemes. *L.* × *adami* (*Laburnocytisus* × *adami*) is a curious chimera resulting from the grafting of *Cytisus purpureus* on *L. anagyroides*, yielding racemes of coppery-pink flowers though yellow and purple flowers may also appear. The tree itself has not great character.

Propagate species by seeds in early spring, varieties by grafting or building on Common Laburnum stocks. No regular pruning is needed.

# Lavender

Family LABIATAE

*Lavandula spica*

The Lavenders are among the pleasantest small shrubs to grow with their square young stems lined with opposite, grey-green downy leaves, and long, upright, slender flower-stalks carrying flowers in crowded whirls forming spikes one to three inches long, and aromatically fragrant in every part. They grow well in any garden soil that is well drained, particularly in sandy loams, and they love full sun.

The Common Old English or Mitcham Lavender, *L. spica*, from the Mediterranean region, grows three to four feet high, with as much spread, with grey downy, linear leaves and spikes of grey-blue, finely-scented flowers in July and August. It has notable varieties in 'Twickle Purple' with long, dark purplish flower-heads; *nana atropurpurea* ('Hidcote' var.), dwarf, compact, and 'Folgate' dwarf to eighteen inches, with lavender-blue flowers. *L. stoechas*, from south-west Europe, grows two to three feet, and is distinctive with purple, bracted flowers, almost bottle-shaped.

Propagate from seeds in spring; by cuttings in summer.

# Himalayan Honeysuckle

Family CAPRIFOLIACEAE

Of the two species forming this genus, only one can be considered hardy, and even then may be cut down to ground-level in severe winters. It is *L. formosa*, the Himalayan Honeysuckle or Flowering Nutmeg from the Himalaya, a shrub of character that rewards one for making a place for it in the shrub garden.

It is distinctive for its stout, hollow, thin-walled stems of vivid sea-green, with six-inch-long, ovate, long pointed, heart-shaped based leaves, slightly toothed and downy-grey beneath,

*Leycesteria formosa*

and notable for its flowers which are whitish and funnel-shaped and hang in drooping clusters enclosed by conspicuous, claret-purple bracts, July to September, giving way to reddish-purple fruits, like small gooseberries, to which birds are partial. It normally grows from four to eight feet tall, and a place should be found for it in a slightly shaded corner where the soil is deep loam, rich and well drained. It is a good shrub for wild coverts, where the berries provide food for game-birds.

Propagate by seeds in a cold frame in February; by cuttings of shoots with a heel in autumn, under handlights. Prune, when necessary, in February.

# Privet

Family OLEACEAE

*Ligustrum sinense*

The Privets number over fifty species, and some of them are handsome enough to be grown as specimens. All have opposite entire, short-stalked leaves, bear small, tubular, white or yellowish flowers in terminal panicles, followed by black or dark-purple berries. They grow quickly, and are easy to cultivate, in ordinary garden soils, in shade or sun.

For hedging or training, *L. ovalifolium* from Japan is best, growing erect up to fifteen feet, with glossy evergreen leaves, and its var. *aureum*, though less vigorous, is the best golden type, its leaves irregularly margined with yellow. For flowering beauty, *L. quihoui*, a Chinese deciduous shrub, of good rounded habit up to eight feet, leads in popularity with slender, long panicles of white flowers up to eighteen inches in August and September. *L. sinense*, China, is a graceful, partially evergreen shrub, growing to twelve feet high, bearing three- to four-inch panicles of small, white flowers freely in July, fragrant, and followed by dark purple berries.

Propagate by cuttings of shoots taken in August, six to nine inches long. Clip hedges in June and September. Specimen shrubs need no regular pruning.

# Spice Bush
Family LAURACEAE

*Lindera benzoin*

This is a race of aromatic shrubs, some deciduous, others evergreen, the leaves are entire and alternate, and the flowers small yellowish, and unisexual, appearing in small, axillary clusters before the leaves. They need a lime-free soil, preferably loamy and well drained, and deserve a sheltered, sunny position to be fully rewarding.

*L. benzoin* (syn. *Benzoin aestivale*) is the Spice Bush of North America, and quite hardy. It makes a shapely rounded shrub of six to twelve feet, with deciduous, obovate, thin, green leaves, and up to five inches long, which give off a pungent spicy aroma when crushed. The small, greenish-yellow flowers appear in dense small clusters at the joints of the previous year's growth before the leaves unfold, in March and April, and on female plants are followed by small, oblong, reddish berries. *L. praecox* is deciduous but only hardy enough for a sheltered, warm wall in a mild district, where it will grow up to fifteen feet, with greenish-yellow flowers in March and April, seen against shining brown shoots.

Propagate by cuttings taken in July or August. No regular pruning is needed.

# Gromwell
## Family BORAGINACEAE

*Lithospermum diffusum*

The shrubs of this genus are low growing and evergreen, with alternate narrow leaves, but to be considered indispensable where conditions are favourable.

The best of these dwarfs is *L. diffusum* (syn. *L. prostatum*), which comes from southern Europe, and sends out prostrate, slender stems as far as two feet, with small, linear-oblong, rough bristly, green leaves to form a carpeting mass, rarely more than twelve inches high, with leafy terminal spikes of stalkless, funnel-shaped deep blue flowers in May. It has several forms, a most popular finely blue-coloured var. 'Heavenly Blue' and var. 'Grace Ward' with slightly larger and slightly deeper blue flowers. These plants must have lime-free soil, preferably well drained and loamy. The roots like coolness, but the plants otherwise like sun, and do well over rocks or down walls. *L. oleifolium*, Spain, prostrate growing, with grey-green rounded leaves, white beneath, and large blue flowers in June; and *L. rosmarinifolium*, southern Italy, a rounded bush with narrow leaves and bright blue flowers in January and February, need warm, sheltered sites but do not mind lime in the soil.

Propagate by seeds, or by cuttings in summer.

**Sh**
*Lonicera*

# Bush Honeysuckle
Family CAPRIFOLIACEAE

The bush or shrubby species of Honeysuckle form a separate section of the genus. They are deciduous or evergreen, with opposite, entire, short-stalked leaves, and with flowers paired on one stalk from the leaf-axils. They do best in a humus-rich soil, free-draining, and in warm, sunny positions, and are quite hardy.

The evergreen *L. nitida*, China, with its small, ovate leaves crowding its dense stems, is much used for

*Lonicera fragrantissima*

quick-growing hedges up to four feet, and var. *fertilis* is its stiffer form. *L. fragrantissima*, semi-evergreen, stiffish oval, two-inch green leaves, and highly scented, white flowers in winter, growing four to six feet; *L. standishii*, also half-evergreen, six to eight feet, with four-inch lanceolate leaves, and creamy-white, fragrant flowers in winter; and their hybrid, *L. × purpusii*, with creamy-white scented winter flowers; *L. syringantha*, six to eight feet, with slender spreading stems and small, deciduous, blue-green leaves, and rose-lilac, sweetly scented flowers in May and June. The Pyrenees provides *L. pyrenaica*, dwarf of two to three feet, deciduous, grey-green, oval leaves, rose and white flowers in May and June, and later, red berries.

Propagate by cuttings in July and August or by seeds.

117

# Climbing Honeysuckles
Family CAPRIFOLIACEAE

*Lonicera
sempervirens*

The Climbing Honeysuckles are best confined to pergolas, arches, trellis and similar supports at the boundaries of the garden, since if allowed to twine up living trees or shrubs there is a real danger of the growth of the latter being constricted and strangled. They are excellent, however, to clothe old stumps or to range in the wild garden. They do not mind shade, but like a moist, deep soil, reasonably free-draining.

Good deciduous types include *L. periclymenum*, the Woodbine native to Britain and Europe, climbing to twenty feet, with green, ovate leaves, and its sweetly scented, yellow-white, flushed red, tubular flowers in clusters from May to September; its best varieties being *belgica*, the early Dutch Honeysuckle, with flowers deeply tinged purplish-red, and *serotina,* the late form, with flowers dark purple outside; all bearing red berries later. *L. tragophylla*, China, ten to twelve feet, is most attractive, with coppery leaves, and large clusters of big orange-red flowers from June. *L. sempervirens*, U.S.A., twenty feet, orange, yellow and red flowers is semi-evergreen and only hardy enough for the south-west.

Propagate by cuttings in July or August.

# Magnolia
Family MAGNOLIACEAE

A genus of magnificent shrubs and trees. With their large, firm, entire, alternate leaves and large, strikingly beautiful solitary flowers, they are aristocrats of the garden, and their culture is not difficult given good, humus-rich, well-drained deep loam and a sunny position, sheltered to the north and east.

*Magnolia stellata*

*M. stellata*, Japan, grows slowly from five to fifteen feet, with white, semi-double flowers made up of narrow petals, in March and April, and has a var. *rosea*, pink-flowered. *M. denudata* (syn. *M. conspicua*) is the Yulan or Lily Tree of China, making a tree twenty to thirty feet tall, with white, five-inch, cup-shaped flowers in March and May, and long, oval leaves. *M. × soulangeana*, (*M. denudata × M. liliflora*) is grown as a tall shrub, to thirty feet high, having goblet-like, white, flushed purple, flowers in April, and var. *alba superba*, white, rosy-purple outside. Of those flowering when in leaf, *M. sieboldii*, Japan, to ten feet, scented, white cups in May; *M. wilsonii*, China, to twenty feet, with pendent, white flowers in June; and the evergreens *M. grandiflora*, U.S.A., fifteen to forty feet, and *M. delavayi*, twenty to thirty-five feet, *Yunnan*, are best.

Propagate by layering.

# Mahonia
Family BERBERIDACEAE

*Mahonia aquifolium*

The Mahonias are related to *Berberis*, but differ in having compound pinnate leaves, which are alternate and evergreen, and stems without spines. The flowers are usually yellow, and are carried in erect, spike-like racemes from the ends of shoots, yielding place to bluish-black berries. They thrive in any good garden soil, including one of lime content, in sun or some shade.

*M. aquifolium*, the Oregon Grape from North America, grows two to three feet tall, with glossy green pinnate leaves, made up of spiny leaflets, and rich yellow flowers in clusters of racemes, February to April. *M. bealei* and *M. japonica* are often confused, but the former comes from China, growing to six feet, with upright, three- to six-inch racemes of yellow flowers during winter; and the latter comes from Japan, grows to eight feet or more and has drooping racemes of fragrant, lemon-yellow flowers, and fine pinnate foliage. Perhaps the most striking species is *M. lomariifolia*, Yunnan, six feet, with leaves having up to nineteen pairs of blue-green leaflets. It needs warm shelter.

Propagate by layering in spring. Prune after flowering.

# Crab Apple
Family ROSACEAE

Linnaeus placed this group of deciduous shrubs and small trees under *Pyrus*, but it is now a genus in its own right. With simple, alternate leaves, toothed or lobed, freely borne white, pink or red flowers in unbranched clusters in spring, and brightly coloured fruits in autumn, they make excellent subjects for the shrub-garden. All they need is a well-drained, ordinary garden loam and full sun.

*M. sargentii*, Japan, is a bush of six to eight

*Malus pumila* var. 'John Downie'

feet, with white flowers, borne freely, and small red fruits. *M. baccata*, Siberia, grows to forty feet, and is the Red Siberian Crab with white blossom followed by bright red fruits. *M. hupehensis*, China, flowers freely with rose-tinted, white bloom, and grows to thirty feet. *M. floribunda*, Japan, to thirty feet, breaks with carmine buds, opening to pink, fading white, flowers, and has var. *hilleri* with double flowers. *M. × lemoinei*, to thirty feet, bronze foliage and deep crimson flowers and is a notable hybrid. For handsome, edible fruits the vars. 'Dartmouth', red-purple; 'John Downie', orange and scarlet; and 'Veitch's Scarlet', of *M. pumila*, are good.

Propagate by seed, if species; by grafting, if hybrid.

# Myrtle

Family MYRTACEAE

*Myrtus*

*Myrtus communis*

From this genus of evergreen shrubs come pleasantly-scented plants for the shrub border. The leaves are usually opposite, short stalked, and entire; the flowers are white and solitary from the leaf-axils and the fruits roundish berries, often edible. As they are from warm regions, they need well-sheltered positions and are best grown against walls, except in the south-west, and succeed in any good, reasonably well-drained loam.

The Common Myrtle, *M. communis*, from the Mediterranean region, makes a well-leafed shrub, eight to ten feet high, with shining deep green, scented ovate leaves, creamy-white flowers with many stamens in July, followed by purple-black berries; var. *tarentina* has smaller leaves and whitish fruits; and var. *variegata*, variegated cream and green leaves. A Chilean, *M. apiculata* (syn. *M. luma*), becomes a fine large shrub of eighteen to twenty-four feet in mild gardens, the stems a downy reddish-cinnamon brown; the leaves small and decorative, oval and dark green; the flowers white and scented in summer, followed by sweet black fruits.

Propagate by cuttings under handlights in July. No regular pruning, but shaping may be done in March.

# Neillia

Family ROSACEAE

The shrubs of this group are all deciduous species native to China and the Himalayan region, and closely resemble the related shrubs of *Spiraea* in habit. The leaves are alternate, ovate, double-toothed and lobed as a rule, and the flowers are five-parted and small in many-flowered racemes, followed by dry capsules, containing shining dark seeds. The plants are hardy and easily grown in any fair garden loam holding moisture, and they like a sunny open position.

*Neillia longiracemosa*

The best species is *N. longiracemosa* of western China, with slender stems, three to six feet tall, somewhat downy, green tri-lobed, slender-pointed and double-toothed leaves, two to four inches long, and drooping racemes of rosy-pink flowers from the ends of shoots in May and June. *N. sinensis*, central China, grows four to six feet, with smooth brown stems, and smaller ovate leaves, and white flowers in small racemes in May and June; and *N. thibetica*, Tibet, is similar, but with downy shoots, somewhat larger leaves, and more floriferous with dense, longer, terminal sprays of flowers.

Propagate by seeds under glass, by half-ripened cuttings in July or August.

# Daisy Bush
Family COMPOSITAE

*Olearia haastii*

The Daisy Bushes or Tree Daisies comprise a genus of over a hundred evergreen shrubs and trees, native to Australasia, but many are of doubtful hardiness. Their attractive foliage of alternate (opposite in a few species) leathery green leaves, white or buff beneath, heads of Daisy-like flowers, and good habit make them desirable plants, especially for seaside planting since they stand up well to wind. They are equally happy in limy or lime-free soils, given good drainage, full sunshine, and shelter from the east and north, or a sunny wall.

The hardiest species is *O. haastii*, New Zealand, a round bush up to five feet, with entire ovate leaves, white beneath, and covered with scented clusters of small white flowers in July and August. *O. albida*, a shrub of six to ten feet, with polished dark green, ovate leaves, much white-felted beneath, and white flowers, July and August; and *O. nummularifolia*, four to six feet, with small, yellowish-green leaves, and white flowers, in June and July, are fairly hardy. *O. macrodonta*, ten to fifteen feet, greyish, holly-like leaves, scented white flowers in June, is one of the best.

Propagate by cuttings in July or August under handlights.

**Sh**
*Osmanthus*

**Osmanthus**
Family OLEACEAE

*Osmanthus delavayi*

This is a small genus of evergreen shrubs with attractive foliage of dark green, shiny, spine-toothed, holly-like, opposite leaves, delightfully scented, white tubular, four-lobed, Jasmine-like small flowers in axillary clusters, which may be succeeded by blue-purple, one-seeded fruits. They are generally hardy, thriving in ordinary garden loams, and welcoming warm, sunny positions with shelter from the worst severities of our winters.

The most rewarding species is *O. delavayi* (syn. *Siphonosmanthus delavayi*), a shrub of spreading, arching habit of six to eight feet, with small, ovate, sharply-toothed, glossy green leaves, and clusters of small very fragrant, pure white flowers from the leaf-axils in May and April, succeeded by blue-black berries. *O. heterophyllus* (syn. *O. ilicifolius*), Japan, is a compact, holly-like shrub of ten feet, with its scented flowers opening in autumn, and has var. *aureo-variegatus*, with yellow-margined leaves. *O. armatus*, China, is handsome, to fifteen feet, with spined, leathery, leaves and creamy-white flowers in September.

Propagate by cuttings taken in July or August. No regular pruning is required, but training or shaping can be done in May.

# Mountain Spurge

Family BUXACEAE

*Pachysandra*

*Pachysandra terminalis*

The species of this group are low growing evergreen, semi-woody shrubs, chiefly valuable for carpeting under trees and growing in densely shaded places where little else will. The stems are fleshy, with alternate leaves, crowded in whorl-like groups at the ends. The flowers are small and unisexual, without petals, and produced in spikes. They are hardy and thrive in ordinary loams.

*P. terminalis* is the Mountain Spurge from Japan, with stems less than twelve inches high, but spreading by means of creeping rootstocks to three feet or so. The leaves are roughly diamond-shaped, with three prominent veins to the base, coarsely toothed to the apex and two to three inches long. In April, small two-inch spikes of greenish-white flowers, tinged purplish, are produced at the end of shoots, followed by capsule-fruits with three horns from persisting styles. *P. procumbens*, the Alleghany Spurge of south-east United States, is similar, but with larger leaves and shoots which are downy, and four- to five-inch spikes of white or pinkish flowers in April.

Propagate by division in spring; by cuttings in June. No regular pruning needed.

# Tree Paeony
## Family RANUNCULACEAE

The so-called Tree Paeonies are really shrubby species of this genus of perennial herbs, and provide glorious colour for the shrub garden. They need a deep well-cultivated, rich loam, regularly mulched, and do best in sheltered positions, but with warm sun in summer. They are hardy but start into growth early, and should be protected against spring frosts.

*Paeonia suffruticosa*

*P. delavayi* makes a handsome shrub up to five feet, with deep red flowers and a centre of yellow anthers in May. *P. lutea* of China and Tibet grows to four feet, with bi-ternate leaves, and yellow flowers up to four inches across, and its var. *ludlowii* has even larger flowers, in June. *P. suffruticosa* (syn. *P. moutan*) of China and Tibet is the Moutan Paeony, growing to five feet, with rather rigid, brittle and hard branching two-pinnate leaves, and rose-pink flowers in May, and has many single and double coloured forms, ranging from white to crimson. Crossing *P. lutea* × *P. suffruticosa* has given fine yellow hybrids in bright yellow, 'Chromatella' and 'Souvenir de Maxime Cornu', scented, very big, bright yellow with carmine edges. Other notable hybrids are to be found in growers' list.

Propagate by layering in early spring.

## Parrotia
Family HAMAMELIDACEAE

*Parrotia
persica*

The two small trees in this genus are both hardy, deciduous species worthy of more appreciation. The leaves are alternate, ovate, and marked with parallel veins, reminiscent of the Witch Hazel family to which they belong. Once established, they flower early in the year, the flowers being five to seven bracts surrounding a head of stamens. They do perfectly well in any good, well-drained, garden loam and open sunshine.

*P. persica*, the Iron Tree of Persia, makes a steady-growing, spreading tree of twenty-five to forty feet, with the bark flaking from the trunk. The flowers are small, in axillary clusters and distinctive in March when they appear for their red-anthered stamens against rough hairy brown-black bracts. In autumn the leaves turn crimson and gold and make an unequalled colour show. *P. jacquemontiana* (syn. *Parrotiopis jacquemontiana*) is from the Himalaya and makes a smaller tree to twenty feet, with almost round, pointed leaves, and flowers of a head of yellow stamens and four to six large whitish bracts up to two inches across from April to June.

Propagate by layering in spring. No regular pruning needed.

# Passion-Flower
Family PASSIFLORACEAE

*Passiflora caerulea*

Out of over three hundred species of climbing plants of this genus, only one is of sufficient hardiness to be grown out of doors, and only in the south and west or on a well-sheltered, sunny south wall. Any good garden loam will suit, enriched with humus-forming material.

The species is *P. caerulea*, the Blue Passion Flower of Brazil and central South America. It is a vigorous climber, growing to thirty feet, by tendrils, and having nominally evergreen alternate leaves, of five to seven lobes, palmately arranged. From June to September the flowers rise singly from the leaf-axils, exotic in construction and colouring. The tubular calyx opens to five greenish-white sepals, the same number of white or pinkish petals, and rings of thread-like filaments, purple based, then white and blue, making the corona; from the centre rises the gynophore or stem carrying the five stamens, the ovary, and the three styles at the top. There is a var. 'Constance Elliott' with large, ivory-white flowers.

Propagate by seeds in February under glass; by cuttings in July. Prune in February or March, cutting shoots back by one-half their length.

# Prickly Heath
Family ERICACEAE

*Pernettya
mucronata*

The charm of these low-growing evergreen shrubs lies partly in their alternate, short-stalked, firm, leathery, ovate and serrated leaves, partly in their five-parted, small flowers like Lily-of-the-Valley, but mostly in their ornamental berry fruits, freely borne in autumn. Like so many members of the Erica family, they need a lime-free soil and rejoice in peat. The flowers are pseudo-hermaphrodite and self-sterile, and it's wise to plant a male plant or two with the females to ensure good berrying displays.

*P. mucronata* from the Magellan area of South America is hardy. It makes a stiff, bushy shrub, two to five feet tall, densely packed with small, dark green, pointed, oval leaves, and bearing small, white flowers from the leaf-axils on wood of the previous year in May and June, which give way to masses of white, pink, reddish or purple berries. Of many varieties 'Bell's Seedling' stands out with larger leaves and bigger, scarlet berries; *alba* has white berries; *rosea*, rose-pink; *mascula*, purplish-pink; and there are others. Other species are only hardy for the mildest counties.

Propagate by layering in spring; by cuttings in August.

# Mock Orange
## Family PHILADELPHACEAE

The Mock Oranges, mis-called 'Syringa', are a group of some forty deciduous shrubs with solid pithed stems, opposite, usually ovate and widely toothed leaves, and white, four-parted flowers, often orange-scented. Invaluable for floral beauty in June and July, but without much grace in habit, their hardiness and willingness to thrive in poorish soils, limy or not are assets.

*Philadelphus × lemoinei*
var. 'Bouquet Blanc'

Outstanding hybrids, such as *P. × lemoinei*, erect in growth to six feet, with highly-scented white flowers, having good single forms in 'Avalanche', and double in 'Virginale', 'Bouquet Blanc' and 'Manteau d'Hermine'. *P. × purpureo-maculatus*, six feet, has purple blotching at the base of its flowers; and in its vars. 'Belle Etoile', and 'Sybille'. Of the species, *P. coronarius*, Asia Minor, grows to twelve feet, with creamy-white, scented racemes, and a golden-leaved form in var. *aureus*. The Chinese *P. delavayi*, to ten feet, and *P. incanus*, six feet, bear racemes of scented flowers.

Propagate by cuttings in July. Prune immediately after flowering, removing branches that have flowered.

In this group there are shrubs and small trees, deciduous or evergreen, notable for their handsome foliage, autumn colouring, and richly-tinted fruits. The leaves are simple, short-stalked, finely toothed and alternate, and the flowers are small and white in short-branched corymbs or panicles, followed by reddish, haw-like fruits. The hardy species succeed in any good, well-drained loam, prefer-

*Photinia villosa*

ably against south walls, and should be planted out of pots if possible.

Of the evergreens, *P. serrulata* of China makes a tall shrub or tree, to thirty feet, with large, oblong, polished leathery leaves, reddish when young, then dark green and turning red in age. The white flowers appear in six-inch clusters in April to be followed by small, scarlet haw-shaped berries, but is only hardy for the south-west. Of the deciduous species, the best is *P. villosa*, China and Japan, a shrub of up to fifteen feet, with slender-pointed, obovate, thin, finely-toothed leaves, downy beneath, small corymbs of white flowers in May, and bright red berries following.

Propagate by seeds under glass in spring; by cuttings in July or August.

**Pieris**
Family ERICACEAE

These evergreen shrubs with alternate, finely toothed leaves are valuable for their white, waxy, urn-shaped flowers borne early in spring in terminal panicles. They thrive in lime-free, humus rich soils, but since they flower in March and April, they should be given frost-free sites, sheltered from drying east winds.

*Pieris* sp.

One of the best is *P. formosa*, China, six to nine feet tall, with long lanceolate, minutely toothed, glossy green leaves, and stiff spikes of nodding, green-sepaled, white flowers, like Lily-of-the-Valley in shape and scent, in May; var. *forrestii*, six to twelve feet, is pink and red in foliage when the leaves are young, and has rather larger flowers; both spread widely by suckers. Japan provides *P. japonica*, a branching shrub to ten feet, with brown branchlets, oblanceolate, pointed leaves, and the white flowers in drooping terminal racemes in March and April; with var. *variegata*, having leaves with yellowish margins; and *P. taiwanensis*, Formosa, erect and rounded to ten feet, with brightly coloured young foliage, and erect sprays of flowers in April.

Propagate by seeds under glass in March; by heeled cuttings in August; by layering in autumn.

The evergreen shrubs of this genus are chiefly valuable for their beautiful foliage and blossom fragrance. The leaves are alternate, in whorls towards the ends of branches, and fleshy with a network of green and white veins. The flowers are generally scented. Being tender, the plants succeed in the open only in mild districts; elsewhere they need the shelter of a wall or cold greenhouse. Any good garden loam is suitable.

*Pittosporum tobira*

Among the hardiest are *P. dallii*, New Zealand, a rounded shrub or tree to eighteen feet, with toothed to entire, dull green, elliptical leaves, and white, scented flowers in June; and *P. tenuifolium*, New Zealand, a tree of twenty to thirty feet, with black stems, pale shining green, ovalish leaves, wavy at the edges, and sweetly leaf-axils, in May; and its vars. Others for the milder gardens include: *P. eugenioides* var. *variegatum*, New Zealand, twelve to twenty feet, prettily foliaged, yellow-flowering; and *P. tobira*, a bushy shrub of ten to twenty feet, from China and Japan, with fine creamy, scented flowers in summer.

Propagate by cuttings taken in autumn. No regular pruning needed.

**Cl Sh**
*Polygonum*

**Polygonum**
Family POLYGONACEAE

The genus embraces annuals, perennials, sub-shrubs and climbing shrubs to over 150 species. It is the last which are useful in the shrub garden.

*Polygonum
baldschuanicum*

*Polygonum baldschuanicum* from south Turkestan or Bokhara is a handsome, quick-growing, deciduous climbing shrub, its slender woody stems reaching twenty to forty feet high, and with its foliage of large, alternate, heart-shaped, blunt- or sharp-pointed, pale green leaves, and feathery panicles of small, white or pinkish-white flowers freely produced from the leaf-axils and the ends of shoots from July to Autumn, it is first class for ramping over old trees or unsightly objects where it can be spread with freedom. It can be grown with striking effect up a wire to the overhead branches of established trees such as Beech, or up a fence wire-netting to shut out an unsightly view. *P. aubertii*, China, is similar in habit but with clear white flowers in somewhat smaller panicles, which may not appear until August. These climbing shrubs do excellently in any ordinary garden soil.

Propagate by cuttings, taking them with a heel, in July or August.

# Shrubby Cinquefoil
Family ROSACEAE

*Potentilla*

*Potentilla fruticosa*

The majority of the species in this group of some 350 members are herbaceous plants. The shrub forms, however, are to be valued for their easy growth and free flowering through summer into autumn. The leaves are alternate and pinnate, and the strawberry-like flowers, with rounded petals, appear solitary or few in number at the ends of branches. The Shrubby Cinquefoils are entirely hardy, and ready to grow on almost any soil, given good drainage, and may be placed in sunshine or partial shade.

The best known species is *P. fruticosa*, a deciduous upright shrub to four feet or so, with shreddy barked branching stems, pinnate leaves made up of five or seven one-inch, pointed, entire lanceolate leaflets, and five-petalled, yellow flowers, produced in ones to threes over a long period from June to September. The plant is found all over the northern hemisphere, including Britain, and there are now many garden varieties, such as 'Cornish Cream', white; 'Katherine Dykes', primrose yellow; 'Red Ace', red; 'Tangerine', orange; and *vilmoriniana*, cream, silvery leaves. *P. arbuscula*, three feet tall, clear yellow, Himalaya, is good.

Propagate by cuttings taken with a heel in late summer.

Prunus consist of about two hundred species of shrubs or trees, alike in having winter buds with many scales, simple, alternate, or clustered, toothed, stipulate, and usually deciduous leaves, five-parted flowers of white, pink or red, and fleshy fruits containing a single-stoned seed. The genus contributes many species of ornamental value, particularly for spring flowering, which are perfectly hardy and easily grown in any ordinary well-drained soil, preferably containing some lime. For the

*Prunus padus*
var. *watereri*

purposes of this book, the genus is dealt with in four sections.

The first consists of the Bird Cherries and related species which bear their flowers in long racemes of two inches or more. *P. padus*, the Bird Cherry of Britain and Europe, makes a tree of up to fifty feet, with oval, finely toothed, and acutely pointed dark green leaves, and three- to six-inch drooping or spreading racemes of scented white flowers in May, followed by small, black and bitter fruits. More attractive is *watereri*, which makes a smaller tree but with finer racemes of up to eight inches long. *P. maackii* is a rare but fine Bird Cherry from Manchuria, growing twelve to twenty feet, with peeling coppery-yellow bark, and flowers in dense racemes in June.

# Ornamental Cherries

Family ROSACEAE

*Prunus serrulata* var. 'Shirofugen'

This section of *Prunus* is one of tall shrubs or trees bearing flowers in clusters and having fruits without a groove or suture. Only the more commendable can be given here.

For February *P. conradinae*, China, is a graceful tree to thirty feet, with white or pinkish blossoms. The cut-leaved *P. incisa*, Japan, eight to ten feet, blooms white in March and April. In April comes the Gean, *P. avium*, Europe, to fifty feet, and its better double white var. *plena*; *P. serrula*, from China, twenty feet, with peeling coppery bark and white flowers; *P. sargentii*, fifteen to twenty-five feet, with large rose-pink flowers; *P. yedoensis*, the Yoshino Cherry to thirty feet, with white flowers, blushing pink; *P. subhirtella*, to twenty feet, with flesh-pink flowers, its lovely weeping form *pendula* and winter-flowering var. *autumnalis*; and *P. serrulata* with its offspring, the Japanese Cherries, of which the fastigiate 'Amanogawa', soft pink; 'Fugenzo', double pink; 'Kanzan', double deep pink; 'Miyako', double white; 'Tai Haku', single white; 'Ukon', semi-double sulphur-white; 'Pink Perfection'; 'Shirofugen', double white flushed pink; and 'Shidare-sakura', double deep pink, carry flowering into May.

# Ornamental Almonds, Apricots, Peaches and Plums

*Prunus*

Family ROSACEAE

These shrubs and trees of *Prunus* are grouped, since they bear fruits with a groove. They flower early in the year, and so deserve sheltered positions from wind.

*Prunus communis*

The Common Almond, *P. dulcis* (syn. *P. amygdalus*, *P. communis*), southern Europe, growing ten to twenty feet, pinkish flowers in March, is finer in its vars. *semi-plena*, *P. × amygdalopersica pollardii*, Pollard's Almond, is a fine hybrid, having rich pink flowers; *P. triloba*, China, six to nine feet, pinkish flowers in April, has a double var. *flore pleno* of charm. *P. armeniaca*, China, the Apricot, grows to twenty-five feet, with pinkish-white flowers in March and April. Among Peaches, the Chinese *P. davidiana*, upright growing to twenty-five feet, with rose flowers in February, and its vars. are good. The Common Peach, *P. persica*, China, pale-rose-flowering in April, has fine varieties in 'Clara Meyer', double rose-pink; 'Russell's Red', crimson; and 'Iceberg', semi-double white. The Cherry Plum, *P. cerasifera*, Asia, grows to thirty feet, flowering white in March, and vars. *blireiana*, semi-double pink; *atropurpurea* (syn. *pissardii*), pale rose; with coppery-purple foliage are noteworthy. The Purple-leaved Sloe, *P. spinosa purpurea*, makes a good tree to eighteen feet.

*Prunus laurocerasus*

The Laurel section of *Prunus* differs from the others in that the species are evergreen and bear their flowers in long racemes. The Common or Cherry Laurel, *P. laurocerasus*, came from Eastern Europe and Asia Minor and makes a quick-growing shrub to a height of twenty feet if unchecked, with oblong, lanceolate, glossy dark green, leathery leaves, to six inches long, and small white flowers in short, erect racemes from leaf-axils in April, giving way to purple-black, egg-shaped fruits. It has several forms, notably *rotundifolia*, of bushy habit, well suited for hedges; *schipkaensis*, with smaller leaves and low growing; and *zabeliana*, suited to banks. *P. lusitanica*, the Portugal Laurel, from the Iberian peninsula, is a fine evergreen reaching to twenty feet tall, with ovate, dark glossy-green, finely toothed and red-stalked leaves, and racemes of hawthorn-scented white flowers, up to ten inches long in June, followed by dark purple fruits.

Propagation of *Prunus* may be attempted by cuttings of firm shoots in July or August; species by seeds. Varieties are often grafted or budded on seedlings of their kind or of related species. Any pruning to shape should be done in summer.

Only one of two species forming this genus is grown outdoors more for its bright colourful flowers than for the round, golden-red, many seeded fruits, which very rarely ripen.

*Punica granatum* var. *nana*

The Pomegranate, *P. granatum*, grows naturally in countries bordering the Mediterranean, Persia and eastwards to the Himalaya. It makes a deciduous shrub or small tree, growing to ten to twenty feet tall, with angled, spiny branches, oblong, lanceolate, entire leaves, up to three inches long, mostly opposite, and scarlet flowers with crinkled petals, one and a half inches across, solitary or in pairs at the ends of shoots from June to September. There are several varieties, notably *albo-plena* with double white flowers; *flore pleno* with double scarlet flowers, and *nana*, a miniature form, with narrow leaves and orange-scarlet flowers in September.

These plants are hardy for south or west walls in the south, but flower better in the drier east than in the south-west. They need a well-drained loam soil, and protection in severe winter weather.

Propagate by cuttings of firm shoots from April to August; by layering; or by seeds sown under glass in spring. No regular pruning beyond thinning weak shoots is needed.

# Pear

Family ROSACEAE

*Pyrus*

Formerly including Apple, Crab, White-beam, Service and Mountain Ash trees, this genus is now confined to some twenty species of small deciduous Pear Trees, with simple, alternate leaves, and small white flowers in unbranched clusters in spring, botanically distinguished in having styles free to the base, and fruits with gritty flesh. They are hardy, and thrive in any well-drained garden loam, preferably in full sunshine.

*Pyrus pyrifolia*
var. *stapfiana*

P. *salicifolia*, the Willow-leaved Pear from south-east Europe, and Asia Minor, makes a small tree of ten to thirty feet, with shoots and narrow, lanceolate, three-and-a-half-inch leaves, covered with silvery-grey down when young, though more glabrous and shiny later, and small, rounded clusters of pure white flowers in April, turning to small, brown, pear-shaped fruits. Its var. *pendula* with drooping branches is highly distinctive and choice, the silvery leaves and white flowers presenting a lovely sight in spring. P. *pyrifolia*, the Chinese Sand Pear, its var. *stapfiana* with larger fruits, and P. *communis* make picturesque trees of thirty to forty feet, with white bloom in April.

Propagate by seeds; by grafting. Prune in winter.

**Sh T**
*Pyracantha*

**Firethorn**
Family ROSACEAE

The Firethorns form a group of evergreen shrubs with spiny branches. The leaves are alternate or in clusters, the flowers always white and small in branched clusters, and followed by small colourful berries or pomes, freely borne in autumn. All species are hardy, and thrive in any reasonably well-drained garden loam.

*Pyracantha coccinea* var. *lalandei*

*P. coccinea* is the Firethorn, native to southern Europe, making a tall shrub or small tree of up to fifteen feet, with small, narrowly oval leaves, white flowers in June, with clusters of bright coral-red berries in autumn; its var. *lalandei* is outstanding, more vigorous and with brilliant orange-red fruits. *P. rogersiana*, China, is of dense bushy habit to ten feet tall, with bright green, oblanceolate leaves, hawthorn-white flowers in June, and orange berries in autumn; var. *aurantiaca* has orange-yellow fruits; and *flava*, bright yellow. *P. atalantioides* is upright growing to sixteen feet, with larger leaves and scarlet berries lasting to the spring.

Propagate by heeled cuttings in July or August; by seeds sown under glass in February. No regular pruning for bushes. On walls, lateral shoots can be spurred or cut back in autumn.

143

The *Rhododendron* genus of over five hundred species and innumerable hybrids and varieties of shrubs and trees, has simple, entire, alternate leaves, with flowers in clusters, usually terminal, bell- or funnel-shaped, mostly five-lobed. They demand lime-free soil, well-drained and rich in peat or organic matter, and welcome partial shade.

The genus is classified in series, of which Azalea is one of mainly deciduous, but some

*Rhododendron molle*

evergreen shrubs. The evergreen Azaleas of Japan include the 'Kurume' varieties, are shrubby to three to five feet, and flower from April to May. Particularly fine are 'Hinodegiri', 'Hatsugiri', 'Hinomayo', 'Kirin', and 'Palestrina'. May-flowering deciduous Mollis varieties and hybrids, grows to five feet tall, with trusses of large, scentless flowers before the leaves. 'Comte de Gomer', 'Dr. Reichenbach', and 'Hugo Koster', are typical. The Ghent hybrids bear tubular, scented flowers as the leaves open in May or June; 'Bouquet de Flore', 'Gloria Mundi' and 'Unique' being very good. Of deciduous species, *R. albrechtii*, *R. arborescens*, *R. calendulaceum*, *R. occidentale*, *R. schlippenbachii*, *R. vaseyi*, and the evergreen *R. mucronatum* are exceptional.

**Sh T**        **Evergreen Rhododendron**

*Rhododendron*        Family ERICACEAE

Botanically, the Rhododendrons are now classified in over forty series and as many sub-series. The evergreen species are invaluable for their foliage as well as flowers, and range from small dwarfs to tall shrubs and woodland trees, mostly flowering in April or May, though earlier or later where indicated. A short list chosen for hardiness as well as beauty follows.

Good dwarfs six to eighteen inches are: *R. calostrotum*, Burma, rose; *R. impeditum*, Yunnan, purple-blue; *R. imperator*, Yunnan,

*Rhododendron orthocladum*

reddish-purple; and *R. scintillans*, lavender-blue in April. Exceptional among the taller-growing shrubs are: *R. campylocarpum*, Himalaya, four to eight feet, yellow; *R. cinnabarinum*, Himalaya, six to eight feet, cinnabar red; *R. haematodes*, China, three to four feet, scarlet-crimson; *R. hippophaeoides*, China, rose-purple, April; *R. moupinense*, China, two to three feet, white, February; *R. orthocladum*, China, to four feet, mauve, April; *R. racemosum*, China, four to six feet, pink; *R. thomsonii*, Himalaya, eight to ten feet, blood-red, March; and *R. yunnanense*, China, ten feet, white or pink. The common Rhododendron is *R. ponticum* of Spain.

*Rhododendron griersonianum*

Hybrids vastly outnumber species in the Rhododendron genus, and to them the gardener may turn for exquisite floral colour for any month from March to August. No more than a representative selection of hardy forms can be attempted here, however.

For blue flowers in May, 'Blue Diamond', to three feet, 'Blue Tit', two to three feet, and 'Electra', two feet, are good. Good pinks are 'Bow Bells', late May; *Loderi* and varieties, May, and 'Treasure', May. 'Bo-peep' and 'Cowslip' are neat, pale yellow flowering shrubs, and low-growing red forms are 'Elizabeth', April; 'Red Cap' and 'Romany Chal' which flower late to July, the last growing tall. Other hardy hybrids from crosses of *R. arboreum, catawbiense, caucasicum, fortunei, griffithianum, griersonianum* and *ponticum*. For May and June flowering are 'Betty Wormald', lilac-pink; 'Blue Peter', mauve; 'Corona', coral-pink; 'Loder's White', white, tinged pink; 'Mother of Pearl', blush-pink to white; 'Purple Splendour', deep purple; and 'Unknown Warrior', red. Hybrids of Azalea series and other species have given June-flowering *R. × azaleoides*, white, edged pink; 'Glory of Littleworth', cream blotched red.

The Sumachs form a group of deciduous trees or shrubs, easily cultivated, and valued chiefly for their ornamental foliage, finely coloured in autumn. The leaves are alternate, simple or compound; the flowers small, greenish or yellow, in axillary or terminal panicles, followed by berries which are sometimes striking. The hardy species given here are at home in any ordinary, well-drained soil.

*Rhus cotinus*

Of those with simple leaves, *R. continus* (syn. *Continus coggygria*), the Venetian Sumach or Smoke Tree, of southern Europe, of eight to twelve feet, with three-inch orbicular leaves, reddening in autumn, and flowers on plumose, branching panicles in June and July, which turn smoky-grey in autumn; its var. *atropurpurea* is similar but leaves and flowering panicles are a rich purple, and *R. cotinoides* (syn. *Cotinus americanus*), south-east U.S.A., forms a shrub, up to twelve feet tall, with large, blue-grey, long-stalked, obvate leaves, beautiful in autumn. *R. typhina*, the Staghorn Sumach, eastern North America, a shrub of twenty feet is notable for its velvety-hairy branches.

Propagate by cuttings in summer; by root cuttings in March.

## Flowering Currant

Family GROSSULARIACEAE

*Ribes*

*Ribes sanguineum*

The genus includes Gooseberries as well as Currants. In Currants the stems are spineless, the flower-stalks unjointed; in Gooseberries, stems are spiny and flower stalks jointed. Both have alternate leaves, lobed and toothed, and small flowers, usually followed by juicy fruits. They are easily grown in any moderate garden loam, in sun or semi-shade. Of the Currants, *R. aureum*, western North America, is the Golden Currant, lax in habit to eight feet, with bright yellow, tubular, scented flowers in drooping racemes in April, then black fruits. *R. sanguineum* is the Flowering Currant from western North America, a branching shrub of six to nine feet, unfailing with its racemes of deep-rosy flowers in April, and soft green, lobed and heart-shaped, downy leaves. Vars. are 'Pulborough Scarlet', deep red; 'King Edward VII', deep crimson flowers; and *splendens*, almost blood-red flowers. Of the Gooseberries, *R. speciosum*, California, grows six to ten feet, with bristly shoots, and bright red, slender flowers, drooping like those of a small Fuchsia in clusters in April.

Propagate by cuttings taken from July to October.

The deciduous shrubs and trees of this group are native to the United States of America and Mexico and provide ornamental beauty in their alternate, pinnate leaves, and drooping racemes of pea-like flowers, appearing in June. Easily grown, they like a well-drained soil, but their branches are brittle and liable to break in high winds and somewhat tender. They should therefore have shelter.

*Robinia hispida*

The pick of the species is *R. hispida*, the Rose Acacia, a shrub growing four to six feet, with pinnate leaves, up to eight inches long, of oval leaflets, minutely tip-pointed, and pendent racemes of large, rich-rose-pink flowers in May and June; var. *macrophylla* has larger, more deeply coloured flowers. *R. kelseyi*, eastern U.S.A., makes a graceful shrub to ten or twelve feet high, with leaves made up of smaller, more pointed leaflets, and flowers of bright rose in drooping clusters in June. *R. pseudacacia* is the False Acacia or Locust Tree of North America, growing too big for the shrub garden, but hybrids making elegant small trees are available.

Propagate by seeds sown under glass in February. May be pruned in summer, shortening overlong shoots.

*Rosa banksiae*

This genus of deciduous shrubs has over 120 species, and thousands of hybrid and varietal forms; having thorny stems, alternate, pinnate, stipulate leaves, five-parted flowers and fleshy seed receptacles or hips. They grow in most soils, given good drainage and humus, and open sun.

Species of bushy habit for flowering June to September, include: *R. centifolia*, the Cabbage or Provence Rose, with double, scented pink flowers, and its var. *mucosa*, the Moss Rose; *R. damascena*, the Damask Rose of Asia Minor, with pink to red, double scented flowers; and its var. *versicolor*, the York and Lancaster Rose. China gives us *R. chinensis*, the China or Monthly Rose, parent of many varieties; *R. hugonis*, six to nine feet, yellow-flowering, but better in the hybrid *R. × cantabrigiensis*; *R. moyesii*, six to ten feet, blood-red flowers and vermillion hips; *R. rugosa*, the Ramanas Rose, five to eight feet, rosy-red flowers, and roundish, orange-red hips; and *R. farreri*, five to eight feet, pale pink and its var. *persetosa*, the Threepenny-bit Rose. *R. moschata*, the Musk Rose, Himalaya, has many bush forms of beauty. *R. banksiae*, the Banksian Rose, China and its varieties like a sunny wall, flowering white or yellow in May and June.

# Hybrid Perpetual Rose
Family ROSACEAE

The Hybrid Perpetual Rose, so popular in Victorian days, originated in France, from chance crossings and selection between *R. centifolia*, *R. damascena*, *R. gallica*, their varieties, and hybrids of *R. chinensis*. They flower in summer and sometimes into autumn, with double flowers, well perfumed and opening flattish, and are hardy. They can be grown in ordinary garden soils without trouble.

The outstanding variety is 'Frau Karl Druschki' with large

*Rosa (Hybrid Perpetual)*
'Mrs. John Laing'

blooms of purest white, shell-like petals, freely produced from June to September, growing to six feet. 'Hugh Dickson' produces long stems which may be pegged down to bloom along their length, bearing large, full flowers, intense crimson, shaded red, and sweetly scented. Others are 'General Jacqueminot', geranium-red, shaded strawberry-red flowers; 'Mrs. John Laing', bearing beautiful soft pink, scented flowers; and 'Ulrich Brunner', cerise-red, large blooms. All make robust bushes up to six feet, requiring little pruning beyond removal of dead twigs and shortening of weak growth. The crossing of Hybrid Perpetuals with *R. eglanteria* has yielded the Penzance Briers, vigorous shrubs growing six to ten feet, with semi-double, fragrant flowers.

# Tea Rose: China Rose

Family ROSACEAE

*Rosa (Tea)*
'Lady Hillingdon'

Tea Roses were so called because their scent was comparable to that of a delicate China tea. They were derived from *R. odorata*, a species long cultivated in China, making a bush or climber six to twelve feet, having semi-evergreen leaves, and large, fragrant, semi-double or double flowers. Developed in France, many varieties prove too tender for outdoor cultivation in Britain. Those worth planting for the perfect shapeliness of their flowers, their exquisite scent and the delicate tints are 'Lady Hillingdon' for a sheltered corner out of doors, bearing long-pointed buds which open to flowers of deep apricot yellow, seen against dark green foliage; 'Devoniensis' a good bush with flowers of pale cream, tinged blush-pink in the centre; and 'Gloire de Dijon', generally grown on walls as a climbing shrub, with flowers chamois-yellow, shaded orange in the centre.

The crossing of *R. chinensis* and its dwarf var. *semperflorens*, has yielded the China or Monthly Roses and hybrids, of which 'Cecile Brunner', sprays of pink scented flowers; 'Fellemberg', rose-carmine clustered flowers; 'Little White Pet', double white flowers; and 'Perle d'Or', orange-yellow blooms, are choice.

# Hybrid Tea Rose
Family ROSACEAE

The hydrid Tea Roses are largely the product of cross-fertilization between Hybrid Perpetual varieties and Tea Roses. They are hardy, free-flowering, bearing semi-double or double flowers in a wide range of colours, more or less scented, and vary in habit from dwarf bushes to tall climbing shrubs.

*Rosa (Hybrid Tea)*
'Mrs. Sam McGredy'

Varieties are legion, and only a nucleus selection is attempted here, according to flower colour: white—'Pascali', 'Virgo'; light pink—'Ophelia', 'Polly'; medium pink—'Grace de Monaco', 'Lady Sylvia', 'Monique'; deep pink—'Eden Rose', 'Prima Ballerina'; carmine, cerise—'Betty Uprichard', 'Wendy Cussons'; yellow—'Grandpa Dickson', 'Lydia', 'Peace'; orange—'Mrs Sam McGredy', 'Bettina', 'King's Ransom', 'Mojave'; red—'Ena Harkness', 'Fragrant Cloud', 'Josephine Bruce', 'Uncle Walter'; bicolours—'Chicago Peace', 'Piccadilly', 'Vienna Charm', 'Rose Gaujard'.

Many hybrid tea roses have sported climbing forms; and many can be grown as Standards, grafted on stems of *R. rugosa*.

Propagate by budding in July; by grafting in spring; by cuttings in November. Prune late March or April.

# Pernetiana Rose

Family ROSACEAE

*Rosa*

*Rosa (Pernetiana)*
'Madame Edouard Herriot'

The use of a Rose known as the Persian Yellow, *R. foetida* var. *persiana*, native to northern Persia and adjacent lands, as a parent plant with Hybrid Tea Roses introduced yellow colouring into the lines of breeding. This resulted in a class of Roses being developed early in the present century known as Pernetiana, later becoming virtually merged with the Hybrid Teas. Nevertheless, this is the primary source of all the yellow and yellow-orange Hybrid Tea Roses, and a few persist in modern rose growing.

The original crosses are difficult to obtain, but 'Julien Potin', golden-yellow, is still offered. 'Angele Pernet', a vivid orange-yellow, shaded apricot, and lightly scented, holds its place, but the line of breeding is best commemorated in 'Madame Edouard Herriot', also known as 'Daily Mail', with its flowers of bright coral red, shaded yellow and scarlet, and highly fragrant. 'Isobel' is a single rose of carmine, flushed orange-red, and 'Mrs Oakely Fisher', rich orange-yellow, is also single. The Pernetiana Roses are hardy and in cultural requirements and propagation similar to the Hybrid Teas.

# Polyantha Rose: Floribunda Rose

*Rosa (Polyantha)*
'Little Dorrit'

For hedges, massing, or freely blooming bushes in the shrub garden, the cluster-flowering classes of Polyantha and Hybrid Polyantha or Floribunda Roses are ideal. Hardy, of compact growth, they produce their flowers freely from summer until autumn.

The Dwarf Polyantha Roses originated in crosses between the small-flowered, clustering *R. multiflora* of Korea and Japan, and the free-blooming *R. chinensis* of China, and a tea-scented variety, apparently unknown. They grow about eighteen to twenty-four inches high, and are easy to grow. A short selection of varieties is 'Baby Faurax', violet blue; 'Coral Cluster', coral pink; 'Ellen Poulsen', deep pink; 'Little Dorrit', coral pink, scented; and 'Paul Crampel', geranium red.

The Floribundas result from crossing the dwarf Polyanthas with Hybrid Tea Roses. Outstanding kinds are 'Anne Poulsen', rose madder; 'China-town', yellow; 'Elizabeth of Glamis', pink; 'Evelyn Fison', red; 'Iceberg', white; 'Fashion', salmon pink; 'Karen Poulsen', single, scarlet; 'Frensham', crimson.

For bedding, they may be pruned hard in spring; for growth as bushes, little pruning beyond thinning is needed.

## Climbing Rose

Family ROSACEAE

*Rosa*

*Rosa (wichuraiana)* 'Albertine'

Climbing roses are usually divided into two classes, Ramblers, and Climbing, Pillar Roses.

The Ramblers are derived from *R. wichuraiana* crossed with other garden Roses, make long shoot growth each year, and remain semi-evergreen. Noteworthy varieties are 'Albertine', scented double flowers of coppery-pink; 'Chaplin's Pink', semi-double, pink; 'Easlea's Golden', yellow streaked crimson; 'Emily Gray', golden-yellow; 'New Dawn', soft pink; and 'Thelma', coral pink, scented. Pruning consists of shortening lateral shoots on the main stems to about three buds in autumn, and occasional on the main stems, more than three years old. The Polyantha Ramblers bear flowers in clusters, and include 'American Pillar', single pink; and 'Phyllis Bide', pale gold, shaded carmine.

The Climbing and Pillar Roses may be sports of Tea Roses, of Hybrid Teas, or of Pernetianas. 'Mme Gregoire Straechelin', pink, 'Zephirine Drouhin', clear pink, and 'William Allen Richardson', orange-yellow, are good.

Pruning should be light in this group, chiefly removal of dead wood and a light trimming or thinning in Autumn.

# Rosemary
Family LABIATAE

The number of species in this genus is botanically in dispute, but the species and its varieties grown out of doors in Britain is *R. officinalis*, native to southern Europe and Asia Minor, but cultivated in Britain for five centuries or more. It is an evergreen shrub, of loose habit and attaining to six to seven feet high, and as wide, if left to grow naturally. With pruning, however, it can be hedge-like. With opposite, linear, blunt-ended

*Rosmarinus officinalis*

leaves, up to two inches long, dark green above, white-felted beneath, and having recurved margins, on downy shoots it is attractive at all seasons, and the strong aromatic fragrance of the plant is very pleasing. The flowers are a pale violet or lavender blue, a half to three-quarter inch wide with a two-lipped corolla, and are borne in clusters of two to three in the leaf-axils, during April and May. There are several varieties, *albiflorus*, which is white-flowering; *angustifolius*, 'Corsican Blue', with rich green foliage and flowers of a bright porcelain blue; and *erectus*, an erect growing form.

Propagate by cuttings, taken with a heel, in August, inserted in sandy soil, under handlights or cold frame. Prune, if desirable, immediately after flowering.

# Ornamental Bramble

Family ROSACEAE

*Rubus*

*Rubus deliciosus*

Among the four hundred species in this group are a few distinctive for their ornamental attractiveness. The stems are prickly, with alternate leaves, lobed and simple, or compound, flowers five-parted and followed by fruits made up of one-seeded carpels. The hardy species are easily grown in any good garden loam.

Those with simple, lobed leaves include *R. deliciosus*, the Rocky Mountains Bramble, a deciduous shrub of five to eight feet, with vine-like leaves, and large, single white flowers in May and June; and *R. odoratus*, North America, six to eight feet, handsome with large, vine-like leaves, and panicles of scented, purple flowers, July to September. Then there is a group with stems covered with white waxy coating, showing effectively in winter, such as *R. cockburnianus*, eight feet, pinnate leaves, purple flowers in June, from China; and *R. thibetanus*, China, six feet, with fine pinnate foliage, purple flowers in June. *R. spectabilis*, North America, four to six feet, has tri-foliolate leaves, and fragrant, purple-red flowers in April. *R. tricolor*, Korea, makes a good ground cover plant, with heart-shaped leaves.

Propagate by cuttings in August. Prune out shoots immediately after they have fruited.

# Butcher's Broom
Family LILIACEAE

*Ruscus aculeatus*

The genus is one of evergreen sub-shrubs, with green stems, alternate, entire rigid, pointed leathery, deep green leaves, with flowers produced in the centre of the leaves from their mid-ribs, followed by red berries. They will grow almost anywhere in the garden, in any garden soil, and do well in shade.

*R. aculeatus* is the Butcher's Broom, native to England and the Mediterranean region, making a dwarf-growing shrub, two to three feet high, with glossy green leaves, and small white flowers of male or female sex, in March and April. On female plants the flowers give way to red berries, and these make a striking picture. Var. *hermaphroditus* is an hermaphrodite form, which berries without the need to plant male and female plants.

*R. hypophyllum* is a dwarf, to twelve inches, with unbranched stems, oval leaves, up to three inches, with white flowers in small clusters of five or six in the axils of minute bracts on the upper surface of the 'leaves', known to botanists as cladodes. It is native to the Mediterranean, but less hardy than Butcher's Broom.

Propagate by division of the roots in March. No regular pruning is necessary.

# Willow

**Sh T**

Family SALICACEAE

*Salix*

*Salix caprea*

Among the two hundred and sixty species of deciduous shrubs and trees of this genus are several of pleasing habit, characterised by branchlets without terminal buds, buds enclosed by a single scale, short-stalked, alternate leaves, unisexual flowers in catkins, and minute seeds with tufts of silky hairs. Hardy, they grow in most soils, but are invaluable for damp, boggy, ill-drained or waterlogged conditions.

Of the trees, the weeping Willow is *S. alba*, var. *tristis*, up to sixty feet. *S. daphnoides*, the Violet Willow of Europe, Siberia and Himalaya, may grow to forty feet, with large, pearly grey catkins along purple stems in spring. Of the shrubby forms, *S. caprea*, the Goat Willow, eight to twenty feet, Europe, is valuable for its golden catkins, known as 'Palm'; *S. lanata*, northern Europe, makes a picture at two to three feet high, with grey woolly shoots, roundish, silvery-haired leaves, and golden-yellow catkins in May; *S. purpurea*, the Purple Osier of Europe, grows to ten feet, and *S. alba chermesina*, should be grown for its stems of bright red, being cut back hard each spring.

Propagate by cuttings in June.

**Shrubby Sage**
Family LABIATAE

The shrubby plants of Sage are few. They are evergreen, with square stems, having opposite, greyish-green leaves, generally round-toothed, and downy with hairs on both sides, and bear two-stamened flowers, somewhat like foxgloves, in pairs or whorls in erect terminal racemes. They make attractive bushy shrubs, flowering throughout the summer, and deserve a good, well-drained loam, a sunny position, and for the more tender species, the shelter of a south or west wall.

*Salvia chamaedrifolia*

The common Sage, *S. officinalis*, of southern Europe, makes a bush of up to two feet, but is best in its varieties, such as *aurea*, compact form with golden leaves; *icterina*, with green and gold leaves, *purpurascens*, with reddish purple leaves, and *tricolor*, with cream, pink and red variegated leaves. Attractive shrubs are *S. chamaedrifolia*, one foot tall, blue flowering, and *S. grahamii*, from Mexico, three to four feet tall with oval leaves having a black-currant scent, and scarlet tubular flowers from July to autumn, given a sheltered warm spot.

Propagate by cuttings in July or August, under handlights. To keep bushes neat and dense, they may be pinched back occasionally during the growing season.

# Lavender Cotton
Family COMPOSITAE

*Santolina*

*Santolina chamaecyparissus*

The distinction of this small group of aromatic, evergreen shrubs from the Mediterranean region is in their silvery-white felted shoots and leaves. The leaves are alternate, pinnate or pinnately lobed, and the flowers are daisy-like without ray florets and borne singly but crowded in terminal stalked heads. They are easily grown in any soil that is well drained, and not too rich, and they appreciate full sun.

*S. chamaecyparissus*, the Lavender Cotton of southern Europe, makes a bushy shrub, and grows one to two feet tall, with stems and feathery, pinnately divided lobed leaves silvery-white felted, and yellow buttons of flowers freely borne in attractive masses in long-stalked heads from June to August. Var. *nana* is a highly attractive dwarf from nine to twelve inches, foliage more intensely white-frosted, and flowers more miniature but just as freely borne. *S. virens* (syn. *S. viridis*), southern Europe, grows to two feet tall, and has somewhat longer leaves of dark green, and flower-heads of pale yellow on long stalks.

Propagate by cuttings taken with a heel in June or July, inserted in sandy soil, under a handlight. May be trimmed to keep compact and bushy after flowering.

**Winter Savory**
Family LABIATAE

The genus is one of highly aromatic herbs, but contains one low-growing shrub which may be placed in the shrub garden for its ornamental virtue, while being of usefulness in yielding its leaves for culinary purposes.

*S. montana*, the Winter Savory, is native to the Mediterranean countries of southern Europe and North Africa; a small semi-evergreen shrub sending up erect stems, twelve to fifteen inches high, with small, linear, entire, opposite leaves, pitted on both sides and with bristly

*Satureia
montana*

edges. The flowers are small and broad-lipped, and pale purple or whitish, being freely produced in the uppermost leaf-axils in axillary whorls to form dense, but slender, terminal panicles or heads. Its pleasant aromatic character makes this shrub welcome at the front of shrub borders or beds.

Propagate by cuttings taken in June or July, rooted in sandy loam, under handlights. No pruning is necessary.

*Senecio greyii*

Of over one thousand two hundred species, this is one of the largest genera, and contains attractively leaved, evergreen shrubs, with foliage consisting of alternate, thickish leaves, silvery or white with felted down, and white or yellow daisy-like flower-heads. They are easily grown, needing only reasonably good, drained, garden loam, and full sun. Their wind-hardiness makes them indispensable for maritime gardens; inland and in the north, warm shelter from searing cold winds is needed.

The hardiest are *S. laxifolius*, New Zealand, growing to four feet, with grey downy shoots, lanceolate, blunt-ended leaves, grey-green above, white-felted beneath, and golden-yellow rayed flower-heads in loose, terminal panicles during summer; *S. greyii*, New Zealand, is pleasing but less hardy, growing six feet tall, with stout branchlets and four-inch ovate leaves white-felted, and one-inch yellow-rayed flowers in terminal panicles in June and July. *S. reinoldii* (syn. *S. rotundifolius*) of New Zealand, may grow six to twenty feet, with almost circular leaves, flowers without ray-florets in June and July, excellent against sea winds.

Propagate by cuttings in July. Prune after flowering.

# Skimmia
## Family RUTACEAE

These small ever-green shrubs are highly attractive for their pleasant green foliage and bright red berries through the winter, and thrive in shade. The leaves are entire and alter-nate, aromatic when crushed, and the flowers are small and white in closely packed short terminal panicles, unisexual in some species, bisexual in others. They pre-fer an acid, well-drained soil, enriched with humus.

*Skimmia × foremanii*

S. *japonica* of Japan makes a bush of three to five feet tall, with ovate leaves, and white, four-parted flowers in small erect panicles, which are unisexual, and only followed by coral-red berries on female plants, interplanted with males. The flowers are scented particularly in var. *fragrans*. S. *reevesiana*, China, grows two feet tall, with dark green narrow oval leaves, white, scented, hermaphrodite flowers in April which are followed by crimson, oval berries. S. × *foremanii*, a hybrid of R. *japonica* × R. *reevesiana*, grows two to three feet, and has normal white flowers in April which become clusters of roundish scarlet berries in the autumn and winter.

Propagate by cuttings in July. No regular prun-ing is needed.

# Solanum
Family SOLANACEAE

*Solanum crispum*

Most of the plants in this genus of over nine hundred species are herbal and of tropical origin, but a few are woody and ornamental in leaf and flower. The leaves are entire and alternate, and the flowers with yellow centres of conspicuous stamens, from the leaf-axils. They will thrive in any good garden loam, in sunlit warm positions and preferably on walls.

The Potato Tree, *S. crispum* of Chile, may be grown as a tall shrub or climber, reaching ten to fifteen feet, with semi-evergreen oval, lanceolate leaves, to five inches long, and with large, open corymbs of purple-blue flowers with yellow centres in June and July; its var. *autumnale* is even finer with more slender growth, flowers of deeper blue being borne throughout the summer. It should be pruned by being cut hard back each spring. *S. jasminoides*, the Potato Vine of Brazil, is a deciduous twining climber, useful for covering tree-trunks, outhouses, or climbing into tree tops, with lobed leaves, and pale blue flowers in racemes from leaf-axils throughout summer; its var. *album* has white flowers. It may be cut to the ground in winter, but with the roots protected, shoots up again.

Propagate by cuttings under glass in July; by seeds sown under glass in February.

**Sh T**
*Sophora*

# Sophora

Family LEGUMINOSAE

The plants of this genus may form tall shrubs or small trees, distinguished by elegant, alternate, pinnate leaves, flowers in racemes or panicles from the leaf-axils, and pods constricted between the seeds. They are hardy for gardens in the south and west and other mild localities, and should be planted in well-drained, good loam and full sunshine.

*Sophora tetraptera*

The hardier species are: *S. japonica*, the Chinese Pagoda Tree, capable of sixty feet or more, with dark green, long pinnate leaves, and terminal panicles of small, creamy-white, pea-like flowers in September borne more and more freely as the tree ages; and *S. davidii* (syn. *S. viciifolia*), China, which is a four- to seven-feet-tall shrub of arching stems, with deciduous pinnate leaves, two and a half inches long, and clusters of pea-like, violet-blue and white flowers from the tips of shoots in June. *S. tetraptera*, the Kowhai Tree of New Zealand and of Chile, is semi-evergreen up to thirty feet, with zigzagged young branchlets, small, oblong-leafleted, pinnate leaves, and half-tubular, golden-yellow flowers, hanging in racemes in May, and its vars. *grandiflora* with larger flowers, and *microphylla* with smaller leaves.

Propagate by cuttings in July; by seeds in March.

# Rowan

Family ROSACEAE

*Sorbus aucuparia*

The deciduous shrubs and trees of this genus are garden-worthy for their fine foliage, corymbose clusters of small white flowers in spring, and for their handsome fruits. They fall into two sections: those with simple leaves with straight veins, the *Arias*, and those with pinnate leaves with curved veins. They are perfectly hardy, easily grown in well-drained loam soils, and thriving best in open sunny situations.

Of the first section, *S. aria*, the native Whitebeam, is a tree of fifteen to forty feet, with smaller oval leaves, flashing with silvery down beneath in the wind, flowering in May, to bear red berries later. The Rowan, *S. aucuparia*, or Mountain Ash, usually grows to thirty feet tall, with long pinnate leaves, white May flowers giving way to scarlet berries; *S. discolor*, China, growing to thirty-five feet, has white or pinkish berries, with its pinnate foliage reddening brilliantly in autumn; *S. esserteauiana*, China, to forty feet, its pinnate leaves colouring in autumn, has its red berries untouched by birds. *S. vilmorinii*, China, has elegance as a shrub or small tree, to twenty feet, bearing rose-coloured fruits.

Propagate by seeds, after stratifying berries in sand.

The genus is one of a single species, closely related to *Cytisus* and *Genista*, but distinguished from them botanically in having a one-lipped calyx.

*S. junceum* is native to the Mediterranean region and the Canary Islands and, as the Spanish Broom, has been grown in this country since the middle of the sixteenth century. Unchecked, it makes a rather straggly, gaunt shrub up to ten feet tall, with long, slender, erect branches and rush-like, green, cylindrical shoots, very sparingly leafed with alternate, linear, small

*Spartium junceum*

bluish-green leaves or leafless; and bearing large, pea-like shining golden-yellow, fragrant flowers, about an inch long, with wide showy standards, in loose terminal racemes from July into autumn. Var. *ochroleucum* is commendable with flowers of extremely pale yellow. *S. junceum* is most rewarding when it is kept back each April, and snipping out shoots after flowering. It grows in most well-drained soils, and is particularly at home on sandy soils, chalky soils and in hot dry places.

Propagate by seeds sown in February under glass, and plant out of pots while juvenile, where it is to grow.

## Spiraea

Family ROSACEAE

*Spiraea × bumalda*

This genus is now wholly one of deciduous shrubs, the herbaceous Spiraeas now being classed elsewhere under *Astilbe*, etc. With alternate leaves, usually toothed or lobed, and small, white, pink or red flowers borne in many-flowered clusters, corymbs or panicles, they are of easy cultivation, being hardy and thriving in free-draining loams, and full sunshine.

One group of species flowers from April to June, bearing white flowers in clusters, racemes or corymbs from branches of the previous year's growth. Noteworthy kinds are: *S. × arguta*, a hybrid, known as 'The Bridal Wreath', a shrub of rounded habit, five to seven feet tall, with masses of white flowers in starred clusters, April and May; and *S. × vanhouttei*, a hybrid, four to six feet, flowering in June. This group should be pruned right after flowering. A second group flowers June to September, pink to red, or white; and fine examples are: *S. × bumalda*, three to five feet, with rosy-red clusters and its var. 'Anthony Waterer'; and *S. × margaritae*, four to five feet, with rosy-pink flowers in large flat heads.

This group is pruned in winter, by removing flowered shoots. Propagate by cuttings taken in July or August.

# Stachyurus

Family STACHYURACEAE

*Stachyurus chinensis*

In this small genus of deciduous shrubs are two species welcome for their habit of flowering early in February and March. The leaves are alternate, and the small flowers are borne in drooping racemes or spikes, followed by round, berry-like fruits. They are hardy, thriving in free-draining sandy loams or peaty soils, and should be given full sun with shelter from the cold winds from the east and north.

*S. chinensis* from western China makes a spreading shrub of six to ten feet high, with greenish or dark brown branchlets, carrying four parted, small, bell-like, yellow flowers in drooping, stiffish racemes in March, with long-pointed, ovate, toothed leaves, having heart-shaped base, to five inches long, and developing small, red-cheeked, greenish-yellow berries by autumn. . *S. praecox* is a Japanese species of similar habit, growing six to ten feet, with reddish-brown shoots which are smooth and shining, and pale yellow flowers in drooping sprays, two to four inches long, a week or two before those of *S. chinensis*; the leaves are more lance-shaped, and the fruits greenish-yellow and a trifle larger.

Propagate by cuttings in July; by seeds in spring. No regular pruning is required.

The plants of this genus make deciduous shrubs or small trees, with opposite, toothed, trifoliolate, sometimes pinnate, leaves, panicles of small translucent white flowers in spring, followed by conspicuous, inflated, bladder-like seed-capsules, responsible for their common name. They are hardy, and thrive in soil rich in organic matter and well drained, and in sunny positions.

*Staphylea colchica*

The most popular species is *S. colchica* from the Caucasus, grown as a shrub up to ten feet tall, with finely toothed, three to five ovate, leafleted pinnate leaves, a glossy green beneath, erect sprays of pure small white flowers, scented as the tuberose, in May, and bladder-like fruits later. *S. pinnata*, St. Anthony's Nut, of south Europe, grows to twelve feet high, with dull green pinnate leaves, and flowers in terminal, drooping panicles. *S. Coulombieri* is thought to be a hybrid of the foregoing two species growing to eight feet, its dark green, pinnate leaves glossy beneath, having a very long terminal leaflet, and with compact clustered panicles of white flowers in May, followed by the typical large bladder-like fruits, it is a graceful performer.

Propagate by cuttings in July or August. No regular pruning is needed.

# Stephanandra
Family ROSACEAE

The deciduous shrubs
forming this group of
plants are of pleasing,
elegant and graceful
habit, with alternate,
tri-lobed leaves,
sharply toothed and
long-pointed, and
bearing small, green-
ish or yellowish white,
five-petalled, star-like
flowers in terminal
panicles up to four
inches long. They
are perfectly hardy,
and do well in any
well-drained garden
loam, in sunshine or
light shade.

*Stephanandra
tanakae*

Only two species
are in cultivation. *S.
incisa* of China and Japan becomes a shrub six to
eight feet tall, of dense, rounded habit, with zigzag,
wiry shoots, with roughly triangular leaves, deeply-
lobed and fern like, and greenish-white flowers,
crowded in feathery, terminal sprays in June. In
autumn, the foliage colours pleasingly. The Japanese *S. tanakae* makes a shrub of five to six feet, with
slender, arching, bright brown stems, and twiggy
branchlets, clothed with bright green, triangular,
double-toothed, sharply pointed leaves, up to five
inches long, and bearing white flowers in somewhat
loose terminal panicles in June. In autumn, the
foliage colours yellow and orange.

Propagate by cuttings in August; by division in
March. Prune by cutting old growth back in
March.

*Stewartia* sp.

This group of small deciduous trees or shrubs has alternate, toothed, ovate leaves, and large, open solitary white flowers from the leaf-axils, with a habit that is Camellia-like. They are welcome for their late flowering in July and August, the rich autumn tints of their foliage, and their attractive smooth, flaky bark. All species given here are hardy for the south and mild localities, and do best in lime-free, peaty loams, and positions affording shade from the hot midday sun. They should be planted young and further root disturbance avoided.

*S. pseudocamellia*, Japan, is a tree, reaching to thirty feet or more, of upright habit, with ovate leaves, and large, waxy-white, cup-shaped, single flowers in July and August. Its compatriot, *S. serrata*, may reach twenty-five to thirty feet, with creamy-white flowers, stained red outside, in June and July. In grace of form, both are excelled by the Chinese *S. sinensis*, growing to thirty feet, with oval leaves, and fragrant, white flowers in June and July, and fine autumn colours.

Propagate by cuttings taken with a heel in August, under glass; or by seeds.

# Stranvaesia
### Family ROSACEAE

The most attractive quality of the ever-green shrubs of this genus is their well-displayed, large clusters of scarlet, haw-like berries, against alternate, leathery, lanceolate leaves, up to four inches in length. The flowers are white, and are borne in large, terminal, branched clusters in June. They thrive in peaty or acid loam soils, and are best placed in well-sunned positions.

*Stranvaesia davidiana*

S. *davidiana*, China, is a hardy vigorous shrub, up to twenty feet tall or more, with entire, dark green, oval, leathery leaves, white flowers in three-inch clustered heads in June, giving way to trusses of bright scarlet berries in autumn. S. *salicifolia* of China, is similar but makes more upright growth to twenty feet, and has narrow, oblong, pointed leaves, with three-inch panicles of white flowers in June, followed by round red berries in drooping clusters. S. *undulata*, China, is a spreading dome-shaped shrub, growing to eight feet tall, with white, red anthered flowers, in clusters, in June, followed by orange-crimson berries in the autumn; its var. *fructu-luteo* bears yellow fruits.

Propagate by seeds, sown under glass in February. No regular pruning is needed.

# Styrax

Family STYRACACEAE

*Styrax japonica*

This genus is one of a hundred species, but only the deciduous small trees or shrubs are hardy enough for Britain. They make delightful specimens, with alternate, ovate, short-stalked leaves, and white bell-shaped flowers, one inch across, in racemes or clusters borne freely at the ends of short side twigs in June, followed by small egg-shaped fruits in a persistent calyx. They are well suited to the open garden in the south and west, but otherwise need a sunny protected wall. An acid loam or rich peat or leafmould soil suits them well.

The hardiest species are the Japanese *S. japonica*, making a beautiful tree ten to twenty-five feet tall, with horizontal spreading branches, lit with hanging, pure white, five-lobed flowers, like open snow-drops, on slender stalks in rows, amid oval dark shining green leaves; *S. hemsleyana* of China, which grows twenty to thirty feet, with orbicular leaves, up to five inches long, and racemes of twenty to thirty white flowers, up to six inches long; and *S. obassia*, Japan, a tree of up to thirty feet, with the largest orbicular leaves of six to eight inches long, and fragrant white flowers in terminal racemes, up to seven inches long.

Propagate by cuttings in July or August.

*Symphoricarpos*

This group of small, hardy deciduous shrubs is chiefly valued for the attractive berrying. The leaves grow opposite, short-stalked, entire or lobed, and the flowers are small, pink or white, in axillary or terminal clusters. The shrubs are completely hardy, but have little beauty of habit, and are useful for growing in shade where little else will grow, in the wild garden, or in coverts, needing only the most ordinary soil.

*Symphoricarpos albus*

S. *rivularis* (syn. *S. racemosus*), the Snowberry of North America, throws up erect roots three to ten feet tall, with small, almost circular, or irregularly lobed leaves, small pink to white, bell-shaped flowers in short terminal racemes in June to August, giving way to white, berry-like fruits, half an inch wide. S. *albus*, eastern North America, is similar, but grows only up to four feet, with pink flowers in axillary clusters in July to August, followed by white berries. The hybrids S. × *doorenbosii* 'Magic Berry', pink berries, and 'Mother of Pearl', white, flushed pink, are good.

Propagate by detaching suckers in March; by cuttings in July; by seeds. No regular pruning is required.

# Lilac

Family OLEACEAE

*Syringa reflexa*

The Lilacs form a group of deciduous shrubs of notable flowering beauty, having opposite leaves, and small, four-lobed flowers, generally scented, and freely borne in terminal or axillary panicles. They are hardy, and are easily grown in rich loamy soil, and like positions in the sun.

*S. vulgaris*, east Europe, is the Common Lilac, up to twenty feet, bearing panicles of scented lilac bloom in terminal pairs in May, and having many forms of which 'Clarec's Giant', lilac-blue, 'Maud Notcutt', white, 'Massena', purple-red, 'Primrose', and 'Souvenir de Louis Späth', purple, are fine singles; and 'Charles Joly', dark-red, 'Madame Lemoine', white, and 'Mrs E. Harding', red, are good doubles. Outstanding species are *S. emodi*, Himalaya, eight to twelve feet tall, long, oval leaves, whitish beneath, white or mauve flowers; the Persian Lilac, *S. persica*, neat and bushy to six feet, with highly scented lilac flowers; and *S. reflexa*, six to twelve feet, with arching panicles of deep pink bloom; while *S. × chinensis*, the Rouen Lilac, is a highly scented hybrid, with several vars., and *S. × josiflexa* 'Bellicent', pink, and 'Desdemona', reddish-purple, are fine Canadian hybrids.

Propagate by heeled cuttings in July or August.

## Sh
*Tamarix*

## Tamarisk
Family TAMARICACEAE

The shrubs of this genus are naturally found in maritime areas, and have slender branches lined with alternate, tiny scale-like leaves which give them the appearance of green plumes; the flowers are very small, pink or white and closely packed in straight cylindrical racemes, often making up large terminal panicles. These shrubs are excellent wind-resisters, for seaside gardens, though they will also grow inland, preferably in good, moist loamy soil, and in full sun.

*Tamarix pentandra*

*T. tetrandra* comes from the Mediterranean region, a deciduous shrub, growing ten to fifteen feet high, with tiny, bright pink flowers in straight spikes from shoots of the previous year in May. *T. gallica*, the French Tamarisk, an evergreen shrub of four to ten feet, with purplish branchlets, and short, slender racemes of pink; and *T. pentandra* (syn. *T. pallasii*), southeast Europe, growing ten to twelve feet, with tiny deciduous leaves, and rosy-pink flowers in racemes making feathery panicles; with a var. *rubra*, having rosy-red bloom.

Propagate by cuttings taken with a heel, July or August.

# Shrubby Germander
Family LABIATAE

*Teucrium
fruticans*

The genus is better known for its plants of medical value. A few shrub species, may however, be used with distinctive effect in sheltered gardens of the mild south-west; their square stems, beset with opposite leaves, and purple or rose flowers being characteristic. They like well-drained, open, loamy soil, and warm sheltered situations in the sun.

The Shrubby Germander of southern Europe, *T. fruticans*, makes a bushy shrub of two to four feet, with white-felted, forking stems, entire, ovate, evergreen leaves, to one a half inches long, and Salvia-like lavender-blue flowers in erect, leafy racemes from June into October, and is one of the most effective silvery-leaved shrubs in its season. It has a var. *azureum*, collected in the Atlas Mountains, with more slender growth, flowers of a deeper blue and more tender. *T. marum* is the Cat Thyme, a dwarf shrub of twelve inches or less, with small, hairy green leaves, white-felted beneath, and rose-coloured flowers, from the Mediterranean region. It is hardy, but attractive to cats and they roll on it.

Propagate by cuttings taken in July or August, under handlights or in a frame. No pruning is needed.

The evergreen shrubs of this group with their spiny stems, and yellow pea-like flowers, are familiar to every country lover. Leaves are absent except on seedlings, where they are trifoliolate and alternate. They are useful grouped to give masses of colour, and to induce free flowering, are best planted in poor, dry or shallow soils, and thrive on broken limestone or chalk, given full sun.

*Ulex nana*

*U. europaeus* is the Gorse, Whin or Furze native to the countryside of Britain and western Europe, growing two to six feet tall, with dense spiny stems, and grooved spines, and bearing its golden-yellow, pea-like flowers freely from March to June, followed by half-inch-long, hairy pods. The double-flowering var. *plenus*, in which the stamens of the flower have become petals, is even more colourful. The Petty Whin or dwarf Gorse, *U. nana* found wild in Britain and western Europe makes a small dense shrub of one to two feet high, with its golden-yellow flowers crowding short, upright, spiny stems from July to October, effective in association with *Calluna*, *Erica* or *Caryopteris*.

Propagate by cuttings in July or August, under a handlight or a frame, or by seeds, sown in pots, and transplanted young. Prune immediately after flowering.

*Vaccinium corymbosum*

The Vacciniums are a group of deciduous and evergreen shrubs with alternate, short-stalked leaves, small, white or pink, bell-shaped flowers, in axillary or terminal racemes, and fruit berries which are often useful for pies, sauces and preserves. They need moist, peaty and lime-free soil, and succeed in sun or shade.

Of the deciduous species, hardy pleasing kinds are *V. arctostaphylos*, the Caucasian Whortleberry of eight to ten feet, with ovate leaves, colouring red in autumn, axillary clusters of whitish flowers in June, then purple berries; *V. corymbosum*, North America, a branching shrub to eight feet, has ovate leaves, pinkish May flowers, and blue berries, and fine autumn colouring, and *V. myrtillus*, the native Bilberry, for good low ground cover. Good evergreens include *V. bracteatum*, China, three to five feet tall, scented, bracted, white egg-shaped flowers, July and August, and red berries; *V. ovatum*, North America, upright to eight or ten feet, with red stems, pinkish-white May flowers, black berries; and *V. vitis-idaea*, a charming creeper, six to twelve inches, with pink flowers and dark-red, edible fruits.

Propagate by cuttings in July or August; by seeds.

# Viburnum

Family CAPRIFOLIACEAE

*Viburnum
fragrans*

Some most beautiful ornamental shrubs are in this genus. The leaves are opposite and simple, the flowers small in branched clusters, often fragrant, and followed by coloured berries. They are easily grown in all but poor, dry soils, and only a short list is attempted here.

Deciduous, the Chinese *V. farreri* (syn. *V. fragrans*), five to ten feet, is indispensable for its highly-scented white to pink flowers in winter; *V. × bodnantense* 'Dawn' is a hybrid with larger flowers; *V. carlesii*, Korea, four to eight feet, is white-flowering and fragrant in April and May; *V. betulifolium*, China, grows to ten feet, flowering white in June, and red berries in autumn; *V. opulus sterile*, Europe, the Snowball Tree, grows to twelve feet, with balls of white June flowers; *V. plicatum* v. *tomentosum*, China, to ten feet, has flat clusters of white June flowers, larger in v. *mariesii*. Of the evergreens, *V. davidii*, China, to five feet, June flowering, handsome fruiting; *V. × burkwoodii*, hybrid, four to six feet, fragrant pinkish-white flowers in April; and *V. tinus*, the Laurustinus of south Europe, to ten feet, blooms December to April.

Propagate by cuttings taken in July or August; by seeds. No regular pruning is needed.

# Bush Honeysuckle
Family CAPRIFOLIACEAE

*Weigela*

*Weigela florida*
var. *variegata*

Formerly listed under *Diervilla*, this is a group of deciduous shrubs, growing about six to eight feet tall, with opposite, ovate, long-pointed, evenly toothed, and short-stalked leaves, and five-parted, funnel-shaped flowers, resembling those of Foxglove, from the uppermost leaf-axils in clusters, in spring. The plants are hardy, and will grow best in good, moist loams, limy or not, with some protection against damaging late frosts.

Of the species, *W. florida*, China, with arching stems, and flowers in deep pink outside, white within, in clusters of three or four in May and June; var. *variegata*, yellow-edged leaves; *W. middendorfiana*, two to four feet with terminal clusters of sulphur-yellow flowers in April and May; *W. praecox*, Korea, five to six feet, with long, rose, yellow-throated flowers in April; *W. venusta*, Korea, five to six feet, with rose-pink flowers in May; and the hybrids, 'Abel Carrière', large pink flowers; 'Bouquet Rose', silver-pink; 'Conquête', rose-pink; 'Eva Rathke', deep crimson; 'Mont Blanc', white; 'Newport Red', rich red; and 'Styriaca', crimson, are rewarding.

Propagate by cuttings in August, by division in winter.

**Cl Sh**
*Wisteria*

**Wisteria**
Family LEGUMINOSAE

This genus is one of the most beautiful, deciduous, twining climbing shrubs, with long, unequally pinnate, alternate leaves, and lone, drooping racemes of blue to white flowers, freely produced. They are hardy, and thrive in good loamy soils, even on chalk, and do best in full sun, trained on walls, pergolas, or old trees.

The finest of the species is undoubtedly *W. sinensis* of China, capable of one hundred feet in time, have

*Wisteria sinensis*

nine- to thirteen-leafleted pinnate leaves, and sweetly scented, lilac mauve, flowers in racemes nine to twelve inches long, in May and June. *W. venusta*, Japan, grows to thirty feet or so, with downy pinnate leaves, and racemes of white flowers, four to six inches long, in May and June; and has a double-flowering var. *plena*. *W. floribunda* of Japan, growing thirty to forty feet, with thirteen- to nineteen-foliolate, pinnate leaves of dark glossy green, and racemes of scented, violet-blue flowers, up to ten inches long; and *macrobotrys* (syn. *S. multijuga*) has racemes three to four feet long.

Propagate by layering in May. Prune lateral leafy shoots by half in late July, and again to two buds in late winter.

# Candles of the Lord

Family LILIACEAE

*Yucca*

*Yucca filamentosa*

This group of American ever-green shrubs and trees, known picturesquely as 'Candles of the Lord', are suited to specimen, courtyard or formal planting. Their leaves are linear, long, narrow and spine-tipped, crowded radially in tufts; and the flowers are large, bell-shaped, usually a shade of white, large, drooping or erect panicles or racemes. The hardy species require well-drained soil, appreciating hot sandy loams, and the sunniest positions.

The best species for most gardens is *Y. recurvifolia*, a native of south-east U.S.A., with naked stem up to six feet, spine-tipped leaves, up to three feet long, arching back, and creamy-white, two-inch flowers in an erect panicle, three to four feet high, in August and September. *Y. filamentosa*, south-east U.S.A., is stemless, with stiff leaves, twenty to thirty inches long, having marginal curly threads, with a panicle of creamy-white flowers up to six feet high, in July and August. *Y. gloriosa*, Adam's Needle, has a short stem, with leaves fifteen to twenty-four inches by three inches, and creamy-white flowers in an erect panicle three to four feet high, July to September.

Propagate by root cuttings of three inches in March, in a propagating frame; by seeds in October.

# Zenobia

Family ERICACEAE

The distinctive shrubs of this genus are deciduous, with alternate, ovate, blunt-tipped, and distantly toothed leaves, and white, bell-shaped, small flowers drooping at the ends of long stalks in axillary clusters in June and July. They are hardy, need a lime-free, well-drained soil, and do best in partial shade.

*Zenobia pulverulenta*

*Z. pulverulenta* (syns. *Z. speciosa* var. *pulverulenta*, *Andromeda pulverulenta*, *A. dealbata*) is native to the south-east U.S.A., and makes a charming shrub growing three feet tall, with its young shoots and ovalish leaves covered with a bluish-white or glaucous bloom, and bearing flowers like Lily-of-the-Valley, half an inch across, in stalked clusters during late June and early July. *Z. speciosa* (syns. *Z. pulverulenta* var. *nuda*, *Andromeda cassinifolia*) is equally beautiful, but differs in the leaves and shoots being green without bloom and the flowers slightly smaller.

Propagate by layers in May; by cuttings in July, August; or by seeds sown in cold frame in October. Prune after flowering, removing spent flowering ends of branches, and some of the oldest wood occasionally.

# INDEX

Classifications in this index follow the style used throughout the book. Thus, a family name is printed in capitals and small capitals (e.g. ACERACEAE), the generic name in italics (e.g. *Abelia*), and a popular or common name in roman type (e.g. Acacia, False).

189